Accidentally Beautiful

The Collective Wit and Wisdom of Autism and ADHD

Accidentally Beautiful

The Collective Wit and Wisdom of Autism and ADHD

Laura Anderson

ISBN 978-0-557-76431-0

To my family,
for your endless love and support:
Justin, for your fathomless depth, mystery, and sense
of humor and Aaron, for your boundless energy,
spirit, and love of life.
You are my source of inspiration and passion.

Contents

Foreword

There are many heartfelt autobiographies written by parents about their experiences raising a child with an autism spectrum disorder (ASD) or attention deficit hyperactivity disorder (ADHD). I have read and enjoyed many of these. But this autobiography by Laura Anderson is different. She writes in a very engaging, insightful, and humorous style. She becomes your best friend, eloquently describing her experiences and how she has been an advocate for her two children. She has learned how to play the system and discovered how "accidentally beautiful" people and situations can be. Her story is not unique, and other parents will identify with the experiences and laugh and cry with the author.

For parents and family members, the value of reading *Accidentally Beautiful* will be sharing emotions and information. It is a feel-good book that will inspire parents and encourage them to become more optimistic and positive. The beneficial effect might be greater than taking medication to cope. This book will improve the quality of life for all family members and indirectly, due to parents having greater energy and insight, improve the abilities of children with ASD or ADHD.

For professionals, I suggest that you read this book with a highlighter in one hand to mark the quotations that can be used when explaining ASD or ADHD to parents or students. My reading of this book absorbed almost the total capacity of a large marker pen. Some of the descriptions are so perceptive: For example, "He's in his own world today and I'm not invited" and "Justin endured perpetual anxiety." As a clinician, I felt that Laura really does understand and is able to explain ASD and ADHD. I fervently recommend her autobiography to both parents and professionals.

Tony Attwood

Prologue

The inspiration for this book stems from the undeniable beauty that comes from being a mother—more specifically, of two very special and exceptional young men. My husband, Brett, and I have the privilege and honor of raising two amazingly complex and intensely captivating boys. Justin, who is fifteen-years-old now, was diagnosed with autism just before he turned three. Aaron, who is twelve years-old, was diagnosed with attention deficit hyperactivity disorder (ADHD) somewhere around his fifth birthday. The ensuing years have brought challenges that have been both an undeniable blessing and, at times, an impenetrable barrier.

When Justin was diagnosed in 1998, the realization that my long-held dreams of what it would be like to be a wife and mother were not to be, crushed me. I had always imagined that, as a mother, I would teach my children the ways of the world: to stay safe, to be polite, and to be respectful. I would help them excel in school: practice flashcards, read stories, and work on penmanship. That would all change now.

When I began this journey with my family, what I did find was more rewarding and intoxicating than my wildest visions had ever been. I knew that I would still help my children learn and grow even with the challenges. What I didn't expect to discover was the many lessons they would teach me. I have learned so much more from my children than I ever thought possible. In fact, I think they have taught me more than I have taught them—and I have taught them a lot. I know things about the world and the people in it that I never would have seen if it hadn't been for my children. I recognize that certain parts of society, which were originally indiscernible, are clear and present for me now and others, which I thought were steadfast, crumble in the presence of children with special needs.

The purpose of this book is to show what wonder and beauty lie concealed in what we are most afraid of: the unknown and the unexpected. Although there is an undeniable loss that accompanies a child's diagnosis with an illness or a disability, there is likewise a disillusionment born in the reality of being a parent of any child. The degree, no doubt, varies. Nothing ever turns out quite the way you planned. What's the old adage: "Life is what happens while you are making other plans"?

When a man or woman becomes the parent of a child with special needs, there is overwhelming grief and the unwelcome, unwanted feeling that you've been cheated. Life couldn't be further from the plans you made, and there is a loss associated with that. There is a natural process in grieving any loss. The trick is to not get stuck in the grief. Staying stuck in the loss and disillusionment robs you of the journey's beauty and the discoveries of the path before you. If you are blinded by the imperfection, then you are oblivious to the miracles, and that is the greatest loss of all.

Mine has been a journey of faith and hope and of belief and revelation. My measure of success has changed. What I thought I had lost many years ago has been replaced by a reality that is far more beautiful than I ever expected to find. Success is no longer about what grades the boys earn, what jobs they might someday hold, or what college they wish to attend (although there is nothing wrong with envisioning such accomplishments). Success is to be content. Success is to be sure of who you are and to be comfortable with that. Success is to be involved in and sustain a relationship with someone you love and who loves you back. Success is a lasting friendship. Success is knowing at the end of the day, that you've made even the slightest difference in someone's life.

The integrity of family life is always a challenge. Every day we face struggles we didn't expect. The chapters in this book provide a lighthearted but entrenched path through embracing the unexpected challenges, becoming an advocate for your child, and finding a way to embrace acceptance and peace. It takes you through learning lessons you didn't think you needed to know, discovering a path out of the entrapment of disillusionment, and finding a way to forgive yourself for things that are beyond your control. The book guides you through creative ways to figure out what works when conventional wisdom fails, to find ways to laugh when it seems improbable, and to look for heroes when it seems there are few. The chronicles in these pages bring the realization that some of the most awesome beauty in the world is found in unexpected places at unexpected times and is quite often heralded by unlikely messengers.

It is a powerful gift to be able to share a brighter perspective and a more endearing outlook. Most of us get so consumed by the incessant needs involved with parenting that it's easy to lose sight of the humor and blessings that abound within the trials. I have found that by looking back and taking time to be in awe of the road we have traveled together as a family, I am able to find a renewed perspective as I bravely look at what lies ahead. By being able to find the amusement every day, it's much easier to see promise instead of the doubt if only for a moment or two.

This book is not a self-help book. It isn't my intention to preach what is right and what is wrong. There are many approaches to life. Everyone's situation is different and deserves its own perspective. I'm not an expert in childhood development. I don't have a PhD, and I am not a celebrity. My qualifications are much more entrenched and more deeply invested because I have the life experience of being the mother of very special children. I don't wish to tell a story as much as I would like to show what a complicated world can look like through different eyes.

The names in these pages have been changed to protect identities, but the events remain delightfully untarnished.

Chapter One

Acorns in the Laundry

Embracing the Unexpected and the Uninvited

There was a terrific cracking noise coming from the clothes dryer. I had noticed that Aaron, my then-seven-year-old son, had succeeded in putting holes in the knees of his last pair of intact pants. But, I hadn't noticed that hiding deep within his pants' pockets were little acorns, which were now ricocheting around in my dryer. I opened the door, and the warm, steamy clothes came to a halt while the little acorns pelted out towards me. Carefully, I looked for dents and chips on the drum, and, feeling some relief that at least there was no visible damage, I continued to rifle through the clothes until, one by one, I collected at least a dozen acorns. Some of them had been still in his pockets; a few of them were hanging by their pointy little tips, stuck to the clothes; and at least one had somehow already found its way into the lint trap.

As I stood there looking at the acorns that had found their way into the washer and dryer, the frustration melted away and left me amused. I pictured Aaron scrounging around under the big oak tree in the schoolyard with his hands in the dirt and looking for treasure. I pictured him completely immersed in his quest, ceasing only when the school bell called him back to his desk. I knew this hadn't been the first time. He had, it seemed, earned those holes in his pants, spending hard hours collecting trophies in the twelve-minute increments of recess.

I wondered what these little seeds meant to him as he carefully tucked them into his pockets and went back to class. Were they alien pods? Were they explosives to protect the front? Maybe they were magical gems of some undiscovered world? Whatever they were, they were obviously a very special prize for one sandy-haired little boy in the shade of a big oak tree on the elementary school field.

Those little acorns just kind of summed it all up in that moment for me. There have been many moments since—and even some before—but that little incident seemed to capture a concept that is so easily ignored and took me a long time to adopt: Don't be so blinded by the obvious that you fail to seek the unrevealed beauty in everything.

This belief formed in me as early as childhood. I suppose I was a romantic at heart. I always wanted to believe in happily ever after. God knows I kissed a couple of frogs hoping to reveal the hidden prince who simply wasn't there, but that never seemed to keep me from looking. I always wanted to find the beauty in the beast.

Although life as a grown-up might be far from our childhood fairy tales, it definitely comes with its heroes and villains, its quests and perils, and even the occasional scary monster. And if all that is true then, I suppose the key to my story really begins the day I met my husband, Brett.

Brett and I met on a blind date arranged by a good friend of mine. It was my office Christmas party, and I can only guess as to whether the holiday cheer, the warm cider and the crisp December evening played a role, but we fell in love almost immediately. We were engaged on Easter and married before Halloween that same year.

Everything felt so right; everything fell so wonderfully into place. We couldn't wait to start our life together. We enjoyed our time together—just the two of us—but we both dreamed of starting a family and knew it wouldn't be too long before we began our next great adventure as parents.

We spent two years getting to know each other and frolicking around like carefree newlyweds. We took little weekend trips up the Southern California coast. We played house and hosted little gatherings with friends and family. We picked out the perfect furniture and artwork. I wanted to finish college, and Brett worked the night shift. Waiting to start a family seemed like a solid plan.

After two years, neither one of us wanted to wait any longer to have a baby. We had effectively embarked on that primrose path of family life. Oh yes, I had heard all the disclaimers: "A baby changes your life forever," "Sleepless nights ahead," and "No more quick weekend escapes with only a toothbrush and a change of socks." How poorly prepared we were. The warnings of the ways the baby would change our lives were pointless because the reality was unfathomable. For example, we foolishly believed that the sleepless nights only existed in the first few weeks of the baby's life. We didn't know they would span decades.

Justin, our first son, arrived into the one-hundred degree temperatures of Southern California in August 1995. He was born on my grandfather's birthday, an adequate and lasting tribute I'm proud to say. He was a big baby, weighing nine pounds, five ounces. He was a good baby; he nursed well and grew strong. He ate incessantly and spit up almost as much. He slept mostly well and seemed to require very little extra of me. But before too long, our unfettered primrose path would prove to be a bit thorny and a bit more arduous than previously anticipated.

Justin has always been a very handsome boy. He has broad shoulders and a long torso. As a baby, he had little wonderful rolls of chub all over. He has these all-knowing sea green eyes and lots of sandy blond hair, which curls up at the nape of his neck. He has a fantastic memory and is quite uninhibited. He is smart, kind, and brave. Justin rarely meets your gaze, but when he does, time can stand still for a moment.

When Justin was about fourteen months old, I took him to the pediatrician for a bad cold. I adored the doctor. He was an older gentleman who had seen it all. I felt comfortable with Justin in his care. On this particular day, Justin and I had waited patiently for him to finish a phone call and come in for the exam. After just a couple of minutes, he entered the room, huffing a little about overbearing moms and late-talking children. I remember him saying with a frustrated smile, "What am I supposed to do? Flip a switch?" I am more than just a little embarrassed to tell you that at the time, it made sense! I remember thinking, *Yeah, what can he do about* that? *Surely there is no medication or treatment to encourage speech? All kids will talk eventually. Some moms just need to back off these poor kids.* And on we went with our bronchitis problem.

Not more than a couple of months later, the good doctor had to retire suddenly due to health complications. I was sad to say good-bye. I didn't know it, but that was a monumental transition for us and would prove to be the impetus in finding a doctor who would recognize a fast-approaching need. This doctor would flip a switch or two to get Justin started in early intervention programs. At the time it was the best thing that could have happened to us.

About this time, when Justin was about a year old, we began to notice that Justin was a bit clumsier than the other kids, even kids who were younger than he was. In fact, I actually stopped going to Mommy and Me classes. During circle time all the babies would sit up or lie down on the parachute while the mommies sang, smiled, and clapped for their little ones. I spent all my time trying to keep Justin's attention on me, while continually propping him up or rolling him back off of his nearest tiny neighbor. Justin was a big baby, and I eventually grew tired of the "hey, watch it, Tubby!" looks from the other new moms. We managed to go until he was about two years old. In retrospect, we should have persevered and forged ahead anyway. I have gotten much better at ignoring looks from people whose opinions shouldn't matter anyway.

At eighteen months old, Justin had started to build a vocabulary. He had acquired only about five words and then suddenly stopped talking altogether. He wouldn't look for me unless he wanted something, and then he didn't look *at* me. He just led me to it. I was mostly a means to an end. There was very little social need for me.

He also didn't respond to me when I called his name. Justin would run ahead wherever we were. One day, a dear friend of mine, an older gentleman, told me to let him go and he'd come back when he noticed I wasn't around. I did, and he never even looked back—not once. This of course sent me sprinting after him before he could reach the end of the long drive way he was trotting down. When we were out in public, I tried to corral him by holding his hand, but he wouldn't have it. He had very squishy, hands with very low muscle tone and no desire to hold on, so it was much like trying to hold one of those water wiggles. His hand just kept slipping away. I held his wrist most of the time. I knew it looked a little extreme to anyone who might notice, but there simply wasn't any other way to keep him near me. I even tried a leash and harness, but he inevitably got it wrapped up in things and around people as he ran hither and yon.

Justin drooled almost constantly—not just when he cut teeth— until he was almost five. His bib was always soaked, and I carried extras everywhere.

He had an insatiable appetite. He was impossible to fill up. As an infant he would drink eight ounces of formula in about five minutes and want more. He would then spit up for the next hour or so. He just didn't get the "I'm full" signal, but I didn't know it yet. When he was a toddler, he would eat anything and lots of it. As he got a little older, those habits dropped off and he became intolerant of most foods and extremely rigid about what he ate. He would eat chicken nuggets, but they had to be from McDonalds. He would eat spaghetti, but it had to be perfectly plain with no butter, no sauce, and no cheese ever. No other form of pasta would do either. Spaghetti meant spaghetti. He would eat plain bread, plain chicken breast, or plain carrots, and the foods couldn't touch each other on the plate. No whipped cream. No ketchup. No dressing. Plain everything. We should all be so picky!

Justin didn't play like I thought babies and toddlers were supposed to. I never realized how hard it would be to play with my son because I thought babies would be easy to play with. That is not to say he couldn't be occupied, however; Justin just preferred to spend time by himself with Thomas the Tank engine or watching his Winnie-the-Pooh videos. He would let you read a library of books to him as long as you didn't try to hold him while you did so. He never colored a picture. He also had a curious habit of grouping his toys into the like sets rather than actually playing with them. I watched him play, always marveling at how he knew which figure was missing and at his amazing tenacity directed at whatever he was putting together. However, he hated to transition from one task to another. Even if he was moving toward something he enjoyed, breaking away from any familiar task at hand was vicious for him and usually threw him into a fit of anxious tears. I later discovered that Justin endured perpetual anxiety, which he had learned to mask, but still it took its toll by the end of the day, and we often all went to bed in tears.

Bedtime was something that did come easily for him. I could put him in his crib after his stories, and he never really objected. He didn't want me to rock him, or cuddle him until he got sleepy. I always thought I had been blessed with a naturally well-adjusted baby. I was proud of myself for raising such a confidant and independent toddler.

Before his third birthday, I learned why all of these things were true and why these strengths and weaknesses were his to own and face. He was diagnosed having a pervasive developmental disorder. To be more specific, Justin has autism.

We had been to see the pediatrician several times between the ages of two and three for the concerns I had and just before his third birthday, she had arranged for a child psychologist to come to the house and work with Justin to try to further diagnose the delays. The psychologist was a kind woman and she and I gave Justin blocks to stack, dolls to dress and feed, and trucks and trains to play with while

Brett watched us. Justin stacked only two blocks because he couldn't balance the smaller ones on top of the bigger ones any higher than that. He got very frustrated with not being able to make a tower any taller than that. We gave him a doll but he saw no reason why she would need clothes or food. And he simply watched the wheels on the trucks spin round and round and round. The trains he lined up end to end as far as they would reach. After over an hour of watching Justin's choices and abilities, along with all the other data that had been previously collected, the therapist told Brett and I that Justin had PDD-NOS, or pervasive developmental disorder, not otherwise specified.

The therapist delivered the news and sat quietly, watching my life swirl around before my eyes and change into something I didn't recognize. I remembering feeling like there was no air to breathe. There was a buzzing in my ears and tingly little lights dancing in my vision. I remember my mouth failing to make a sound and my brain being unwilling to help me form thoughts. My world swam around in my head while I watched Justin line up the trains he loved so dearly. I remember being aware that Brett was still beside me. I had done enough research to know what I was hearing. Brett was still blissfully ignorant for a few moments longer than I. I remember feeling like I was being consumed by a river of knowledge which was drowning me, while he was happily unaware on the shore. Then I commanded my dry throat to help me slowly explain what she meant.

The National Dissemination Center for Children with Disabilities (NICHY) gives the following criteria to define the parameters of autism:

> Some or all of the following characteristics may be observed in mild to severe forms:
>
> - Communication problems (e.g., using and understanding language),
> - Difficulty relating to people, objects, and events,
> - Unusual play with toys and other objects,
> - Difficulty with changes in routine or familiar surroundings, and
> - Repetitive body movements or behavior patterns

Children with autism, or pervasive developmental delays, vary widely in abilities, intelligence, and behaviors. Some children do not speak; others have language that often includes repeated phrases or conversations. Children with more advanced language skills tend to use a small range of topics and have difficulty with abstract concepts. Repetitive play skills, a limited range of interests, and impaired social skills are also generally evident. Unusual responses to sensory information—for example, loud noises, lights, and certain textures of food or fabrics—are also common.

When Justin was diagnosed, I didn't realize how the prevalence of autism has exploded in the last ten years. For decades before the 1980's autism was considered rare and the Center for Disease Control (CDC) had said that autism was estimated to affect one in every 2000 children (1)(2). In 1998—when autism entered our world—the incidence of autism, I learned, was about one child in five hundred children.

In 2010 the latest CDC report shows the incidence of autism and related diagnoses has risen to one in 110 children in the United States (3). By comparison, the incidence of children born with cerebral palsy is about one in 250 (4), and the incidence of children born with Down's syndrome is about one in eight hundred (5). These statistics are staggering. Even allowing for misdiagnoses, bandwagon diagnoses, and a better understanding of the disorder's parameters, the steady and unfaltering increase is incredible.

Three out of four children diagnosed are boys although there seems to be some indication that girls who are high functioning might be able to mask the disorder better and, therefore, remain undiagnosed. Dr. Tony Atwood, one of the leading clinicians in the field of high-functioning autism and the related Asperger's disorder, indicates (6) that girls may establish better coping mechanisms which camouflage the traits affiliated with the disorders. Girls might often be better at scripting, or acting out a socially acceptable role that they have learned through intellect rather than intuition. Dr. Atwood also has noted that girls are more likely than boys to be guided and protected by same gender peers, and they are more likely than boys to form a close friendship with someone who demonstrates a mothering type of attachment. There is not a *failure* then to form a meaningful relationship, but the bond that is formed lacks depth and quality.

Some of the characteristics of autism make many scholars believe that Justin stands in elite company. It is believed, though impossible to prove because they are deceased, that Albert Einstein, Thomas Jefferson, Wolfgang Amadeus Mozart, Sir Isaac Newton, and Nikolai

Tesla, to name a few, were all to some degree, autistic. They were all geniuses but social misfits nonetheless. It wasn't merely their profound talents and intelligence that set them apart but their inability to fold neatly into polite society. Many convincing accounts of their social missteps and idiosyncrasies are given in books such as *Diagnosing Jefferson, Different Like Me,* and *Asperger's and Self-Esteem: Insight and Hope Through Famous Role Models.*

Brett and I dealt with the change to our world in different ways. I was scared. I cried. I swore. I got angry at God. I pleaded. I prayed. I took long baths. I asked for answers that didn't exist. But I packed all of that into the evenings after Justin had gone to bed, and I was alone in the house. Brett went to work. If he felt broadsided, he never let on. He didn't seem to fathom the gravity of the situation. I felt alone in my grief.

I remember one evening in particular that the understanding began sinking in just a little bit farther for me. Brett and I were expecting our second child and I was quietly contemplating the new little person growing inside. I hadn't met Aaron yet, and that scared me even more. A terrifying realization rose up and it dawned on me that Aaron too, may be on the spectrum. I was already 6 months along when Justin was diagnosed. I was already well on my way to an even more complicated future. I also remember a feeling of peace as I realized that at the very least, I already knew the steps to this dance. I knew what to watch for. I knew who to contact. I knew how to get help and when. I would be fine if Aaron had the same challenges. We would be fine. I felt like I could handle it, I could help Justin, I could help Aaron, and I could show Brett how to cope, that everything would be fine.

A couple of months later Aaron joined our little threesome in September 1998. He arrived six weeks after Justin turned three. He stripped Justin of his heavyweight title and tipped the scales at nine pounds, fifteen and a half ounces and measured twenty-two inches long. He didn't hold this claim to fame for long. He grew well but was wiry and lean of stature. Aaron was a vocal baby and never one to take the backseat for long. He rounded out our family perfectly.

I held on tightly to all the stories I read of all the famous role models and had to believe that there was a future for Justin. I tried to remember that so many of the people we recognize as significant contributors to science and industry were definitely quirky by nature, and probably somewhere on the spectrum. So hand in hand with these ego boosting heroes of long ago, the four of us would embark together on this tangled journey of discovery, frustration, and enlightenment. Early on I worried all the time about how much time I needed to spend with Justin at therapies and because of that baby Aaron would miss out. I was afraid I wouldn't have time or energy to engage him enough one on one. It didn't take me too long to realize that was never going to happen.

Aaron is kinetic and a constant energy force. Like the sun. He is a delight, but he is incessant. Aaron made sure he engaged me, and so if anything, I had to be intentional to stay plugged in with Justin because Justin was happy enough left by himself. I had to work at social interactions with him. For Aaron, it just came naturally and without coercion.

Both boys had to be watched every minute, but Aaron was his own worst enemy. I don't think the moms of the little girls at preschool thought he was so harmless either. Some of their cute little daughters got pretty good at ducking and covering as their towers of wooden blocks came tumbling down around them. Why would a preschool have large solid wooden blocks anyway? Surely Aaron wasn't the only rowdy child the preschool had ever had? But Aaron proved challenging; he went through three preschools before he started kindergarten. We were not ever asked to leave, but we never found a place that knew how to work with him. No one at the preschools seemed interested in taking him on. It was a pity because he was, and is, so alarmingly bright.

Aaron is beautiful. He has big green eyes framed by a ring of long, dark lashes, a wicked little arch to his eyebrows and an innocent smile that says, "Surely, you don't mean me?" He has straight sandy brown hair, which turns blond in the sun, and slightly pointed ears that stick out just a touch, giving him an elfish charm. He can be the sweetest, most kind-hearted little boy you could ever hope to meet, but he also finds endless ways to challenge himself and all of us who love him.

It wasn't long before we would discover why he craved constant movement and collisions, loved the gooey mediums of paint and clay and glue, and couldn't ever seem to unwind. It was only the beginning of the path that would lead us through the tangle of discovering the joys of attention deficit hyperactivity disorder alongside autism. We had two boys with two developmental challenges and a whole world of entangled blessings.

Someone once told me that life should be lived to the fullest: Love big, laugh big, and live big. Basically be animated, be dramatic, be upset, be in love, and do it with your whole heart. I'm glad someone thinks so. It's reassuring to hear although it can be exhausting for every little thing to matter so much, especially when it comes to my two boys. I am sure it is a good experience for both of them to live so large, but it is a challenge to get their feet firmly back on the ground without trial and tears. That unwinding part is a bear. It is not unlike what you might describe as coming down off a high. Like recuperating after a day spent at Disneyland, everyday! There is a lot of work that goes into every part of life around here.

For Justin, we label everything. We have spent years putting words to feelings, reactions, and faces. We try and show him what facial expressions mean; we try to describe feelings and look for ways to give him visual cues to set them in his mind. For Aaron, we spend time decompressing and then talking through the ups and downs. We try to provide ample time and space to burn off energy and let him soar.

There is a role for everyone. While Justin might have a difficult time reading faces and body language that show emotion and reaction, Aaron does his part and then some at making faces that leave *no* doubt what's running through his mind! He has the best "I'm infuriated" face that I have ever seen, and likewise, his smile can light up a room. We all seem to provide each other with ample experiences from which to learn and grow.

Like a lot of kids, Justin and Aaron participate in extracurricular activities. Although most kids I know are allowed to play sports, take up scouting, play a role in a stage production, or whatever seems to suit them so long as their grades or academic achievements don't falter, for my boys, these activities seem to be far more critical. Society says that social gatherings are second to the skills they learn at school, which thankfully besides reading, writing, and 'rithmatic, also includes random access memory. Computer skills are going to be instrumental to their success. At our house it's those extracurricular activities that are more vital a focus. Those are so much harder to figure out.

Social gatherings offer a far greater challenge than any textbook operation ever will. Improper fractions, the discovery of the New World, and the ability to make a natural disaster out of newspaper and baking soda will always have their places, but the real challenge lies in making day-to-day social nuances clear enough for Justin. Although I doubt anyone will ever really care if Justin forgets how to multiply integers or can't recall the precise year of the Bolshevik Revolution, I have a strong suspicion that nearly everyone will insist that he remembers to wait his turn in line, that we do not all necessarily want to once again relive the evolution of strange little Japanese anime cartoon characters of various abilities, and that in mixed company he really does need to be fully clothed before he enters the room.

Both boys have outstanding memories and adequate skills to keep the teachers impressed and at bay. Even so class work and homework are actually quite difficult to complete—not because of the content, but because it requires not just focus and fine motor skills but organization and creativity. These are things that prove to be elusive goals most of the time. So although the school day is a great challenge for them both, it is the after-school activities that build the long-term foundations that they will need. Cub Scouts, karate, and soccer offer continuous, unpredictable social eruptions and tangles of peer interaction that they must learn to handle. Although for most of the typical world these things will continue to be privileges, for Justin and Aaron they are a necessary part of their education and growth because so many of social rules can't be taught except through experience.

The days seem almost endless. The days seem to spin by like those teacups at Disneyland. It is exhausting and occasionally nauseating. One learning experience after another whizzes by while you do your best to guide the situation and pull it out of its spin only to be greeted by the next sharp loop. Brett and I would try to be proactive about every detail and create circumstances from which the kids could succeed instead of falter. For example, instead of fighting every night about going to bed, we gave them the tools to work through the steps. Every night we would work our way through the bedtime chart, using stickers to mark each step. *Use the toilet*, check! *Take a bath*, check! *Brush teeth*, check! *Put on Grandma Becky's made-to-order night train PJs*, check! *Read stories*, check! And so the bedtime shuffle would go. It was draining. At the end of most days, I often had little sensation left in my body and mind—unless you count vertigo, of course.

Every day seems full, from the early morning struggle out the door to the reading and answering of communications from Justin's aide, from the high stretch kicks at karate to the Cub Scout Webelos bridging ceremonies, and then from the fits and tears of homework to the ever-lengthening bedtime routine.

A typical day would find Brett in bed until 11:00 AM following his swing shift at the post-production studio in Hollywood. I would be up by 7:00 AM to get the boys off to school and then myself off to work at the veterinary hospital as the manager and a part-time technician. It was a perfect place to be a grown-up. I could escape the heavy weight of what home was. It wasn't less demanding, but it was just demanding in a different way. It was much more physically and intellectually but less emotionally demanding. It was my favorite respite. I had been a technician for thirteen years since I was seventeen years old, and I was very good at it. I was the go-to girl here, too.

I left work by 2:30 PM so that I could get across town in time to pick up the boys from school. We stopped by home to see Brett for an hour or so until he had to leave for work. At 4:30 PM Brett was off to work, and the boys and I were left to our afternoon and evening routine. Every day we had one therapy or another, a sports practice or game, or a scouting meeting. We always had homework, dinner, and bedtime to get through.

Every day started and ended without Brett. He seemed to have a pretty easy gig if you ask me. At work he would sit in a room alone surrounded by high-tech equipment, an endless supply of coffee, and a state-of-the-art sound system to keep him company. He worked late but came home to a quiet house. He could sleep as late as he chose to. He rarely had to look after anyone or clean anything up. He ate at a leisurely pace, padded about, or ran errands he wanted to do, and he did it all unassisted with no little helping hands. No, I didn't feel sorry for him. Going to work sounded blissful.

Brett reminded me that he wasn't running out on the evenings' demands because he was going to work to support his family. I knew this, of course, but somehow I still resented that I was always the only one of us who ever had to attend to all these needs. He had days and nights almost entirely to himself, and I was just a tad jealous.

He saw the boys and me for an hour or two at the most and at the only point in the day, which allowed for a bit of recreation, that short span of time after school and before the next segment of the day.

Brett would admire the kids or play with them and then head off to work, but on those weekend occasions when we would be out, he had no idea how to be a parent to these two challenging children. He loved the boys, but he didn't understand them or his role with them.

Every night after the kids were finally asleep and before I fell asleep, I would call Brett at work to say good night and try to find a minute or two to connect although the more I shared, the less he understood and the more withdrawn he became. Brett worked for a post-production film studio, transferring film to video and DVD. He was a colorist and spent endless hours changing and enhancing colors and images before the final product went to post-production. I tried to be sympathetic to his frustrations at work, having to redo images on the twenty-year-old flicks and having to sync up audio to video images, but the truth was I didn't care. His world and his worries seemed so removed from mine that we rarely seemed to find any common ground. In some ways it seemed easier to be a single parent at least in practice, but that thought wasn't very conducive to a healthy relationship because too much resentment builds up and eats away at the foundation

Brett also began to resent that I didn't have enough time for him. He resented that the boys required so much of me. It's really no wonder that what Brett and I relish most is a few hours to ourselves or perhaps even a weekend away in some little pine tree mountain nook every so often. It really is startling to look at your spouse, who you have lived with for years, and realize that you barely know who he is. How does that happen? How do two little kids who can barely tie their shoes manage to tie us into knots? How do these little boys who can just barely keep their balance without training wheels manage to steer us so commandingly off course? How fragile and imperative this balance is between two growing boys, who need our unfaltering attention and undying devotion, and two loving parents and friends, who try to keep the tensile bonds of marriage intact and poised. The distance that arose from his absence and conflicting schedule started to creep in.

It was no real surprise that Brett and I finally ended up in counseling. I was fortunate that he was willing to go. The circus routine spun out of control, and all those little plates I was trying to keep spinning on the ends of the broom handles started to crash down around us and shatter on the floor at our feet. I didn't have enough energy to keep up the crib notes approach for Brett, and he didn't have the time to delve deeply into the inner workings of all of the issues that faced us every day. He resented that the boys were so all consuming and probably felt his footing slip in the lineup. Without question, the pecking order was out of whack. Brett and I always came second. We had a lot of trouble finding ways to sneak out for dates because it was very, very difficult to find someone we trusted and didn't want to lean too heavily on anyone who would come and watch the kids on a regular basis. It was a tall order for anyone, especially at bedtime. Our relationship began to show signs of wear and slowly began to unravel.

Some days it is easy to get stuck in too much reality. Some days it is hard to find the humor and the promise. One day as I wait outside the school, Aaron comes storming up to the car. I cringe just a little at the events that are already playing out in my mind. I know that look, and it doesn't hold much promise for peace and ease this afternoon. I know something went wrong today: Someone hurt his feelings or he ran out of time on his -12s test. There will be civil unrest to follow because I seem to be a safe place to unload. *Will we get through two pages of homework, a nutritionally balanced dinner, a Cub Scout meeting, and unwind time with Judy Blume? Will we be able to unmask the evildoer of the day so that we can sort it out and let it go?* The door opens, and Aaron's lunch bag whistles past my ear and hits the window. He is seething and slams his body into his seat and fights with the seat belt.

Somehow my usual greeting of "How was today?" seems misplaced and ill advised. I think my dinner plans have just changed because my child needs me more than the chicken does tonight.

It is very hard on those occasions when the director of the preschool wants to schedule a surprise parent–teacher conference to discuss the recent behavioral concerns and the second grade teacher points out that your elder son decided to turn his desk upside down in the middle of class, it makes for a long day. When Aaron can't organize his mind long enough to retain his counting skills or his ABCs and Justin misinterprets all the social banter on the playground and swings his pool queue menacingly before jumping the fence to head for home. On these days you make oatmeal for dinner. Some days the calming words that I whisper to my children as they snuggle down to sleep—"Tomorrow is a new day"—somehow reverberates around in my head more like a threat than a comfort, and I can only hope that these words fell upon their ears in the way I intended and in not the way they sounded to me. Some days the sight of the morning sun is too much to bear. These days in a room full of people, it is quite possible to feel totally alone.

Throughout the years, I have addressed Christmas cards, and I have wondered what each of these families is really like behind the holiday cheer. *Are they really those shining well-mannered faces that come in the pictures tucked inside the card? How many shots did it take to get the one that came in the mail?* I'm convinced they are all digitally mastered. Do you know what it is like to try to get both of my boys in a picture together? I have given up. I send one of each now. Perhaps there will come a year when they don't make each other's idiosyncrasies ignite, but I know it isn't going to be this year; that much is a fact. I have a suspicion that I'm not alone in these queries. I have a feeling that every parent at one time or another has wondered the same thing. Each one of us from time to time feels the need to scream, if only inside, "How did I get here?"

I never imagined I would spend endless hours trying to teach my child to talk, jump, and play, and by doing so, I would tap into a level of connection that a lot of parents never know. I feel privileged at having been present at a miracle when Justin spoke a sentence for the first time: "Yook monnie, a dig geen tuck!" which meant, "Look Mommy, a big green truck!" It doesn't look like much on paper, but it's a masterpiece when set to the orchestration of the years of work that had preceded it.

Moments like that redefine my measure of success. What I thought had been lost has been replaced by a reality that is more beautiful than anything I could have envisioned. (I think any parent recognizes that his or her children are not the ones they read about in the books or watched in *Little House on the Prairie* reruns. And most of us remember things about our own childhoods that we *still* hope our parents never discover.) As parents, we all discover along the way that every child needs extra help in some way although I have met a few children that seem to take very little energy. For example, Justin might have trouble understanding the intricacies of friendship, but by age six he understood the relationship of symbiosis. Aaron might have trouble quieting his mind to complete assignments, but he can shoot a hockey puck into the goal off a pass from his dad.

Looking back, this wasn't what I had planned, but I put away all the books about what to expect when raising children a long time ago. They just were not written with my circumstances in mind.

My greatest fear isn't what my children won't accomplish in life, but is what I might miss in the journey as they work toward whatever their accomplishments might be.

For example, when I watch them sleep at night and am lucky enough to see that Aaron has finally faded off before I crumple into bed, I fight the urge to think they are just recharging. I allow myself just a minute to wonder what joyful magical moments they might bring tomorrow when they own an accomplishment like when Justin graduated from elementary school. There were kids whose grades were better, who put more detail into their work, who had more friends, or who did better on the state tests, but there wasn't one among them who worked harder or accomplished more than he did. His victory was his own, but I relished in it just a bit myself. These accomplishments can be big or small, but the magnitude doesn't make them any less magical.

So let's go back to the beginning. What do you do with a handful of perfectly washed acorns? There I stood looking at these sharp, smooth, shiny little seeds. *Have they been abandoned by their owner, or are they a treasure to be reclaimed?* I turned a few of them over in my palm, admiring them and imagining the care and work that went into their harvest. I thought about Aaron scrounging around hurriedly with dust clouds rising up around him, as he tried to find as many as he could before the bell—ending his search and calling him back to class—rang. It suddenly became clear why his hands always looked as they did upon his return home. Somehow the beauty of this unexpected treasure became clear. Each little revelation brought me a little closer to finding beauty in the chaotic abyss. Somehow it wasn't too hard to understand that these little acorns were destined to be something great. They might one day become a great oak, or they might remain the vessel of a child's imagination. Either way, they were already more than they had appeared to be.

I put the acorns on Aaron's dresser where he would find them when he got home. They were next to his rocks, an old bone of some sort, and some bright-colored little plastic beads that he had found on his archeological digs. I sat there on the edge of his bed and looked around his room. It was full of little collections and trophies. So how could something so insignificant be so powerful? How could it be that something so unexpected and initially maddening brought an entirely new focus to the day? These were not just acorns, of course; these were little boys in clever disguise. They were reminders that I had not found what I had expected to when I started this journey.

Chapter Two

IEP–Idealistic Expectations and Promises

Becoming an Advocate

It was the day before I was due to give birth to Aaron, and I sat uncomfortably in a steel-framed chair at a long table in the school district's main office. We were meeting to develop Justin's Individual Education Plan (IEP), an overview of any developmental delays that had occurred and an establishment of measurable goals and objectives for the year. Many professionals—those involved in the education of a child with special needs and each with their own area of expertise—attend. They list off all the areas of need and then attempt to explain what magic they will work to make sure your child makes strides toward greatness. I had been thoroughly warned about the overwhelming nature of IEPs. Although I took some comfort in that the state's Regional Center program for early intervention would still help with social development, I was concerned that the school district was now responsible for his education because others had told me how difficult it could be to work with bureaucratic school districts. I entered into this meeting with terror reigning and pronounced naiveté.

My protruding abdomen would not allow me to move close to the table so I did what I could to look intent and intelligent. I tried to lean as far in as possible without letting on how uncomfortable I really was. I felt ready to split at the seams, but I tried to hide it so that I could be taken seriously. I knew this meeting would be vital to see what challenges that Justin, now three, would face in the coming year.

The meeting flowed around me. My side surrounded me: Justin's case worker from the Regional Center, his inclusion consultant, and Brett. Opposite us sat their side: the district representative, who was also a psychologist and in charge of pupil services, the occupational therapist, the speech and language pathologist, and the adaptive PE teacher. Everyone gave their report about how Justin had performed on their various rating scales and assessment tests. The therapists reported on how delayed his fine and gross motor skills were, how many years behind his speech was, how absent his social skills and self-help skills were, and how different he was from his typically developing peers. It was painful to hear.

They presented me with page after page of what his goals should be, what the measurable objectives for these goals were, and how they proposed to meet these needs. They told me how many times a week he would receive occupational therapy (OT), speech, adaptive PE, inclusion support, and have access to the Resource Center for test taking or for further individual support. They told me that he seemed happy and to be making progress in his current preschool, and the district suggested that he remain there. They didn't recommend their special day class preschool, for which I was relieved. I had wanted him to stay with typical peers in the hopes that he would begin to adopt age-appropriate characteristics and language. If he had any hopes of mimicking typical behavior, I felt he had better be surrounded by it.

The meeting ended, and all had seemed to go well despite my worries. I had heard how difficult it could be to get what your child needed. I had been prepared to stand firm for what I thought he needed and to fight because they would try to take away things that were already in place. They did not; they seemed eager to help Justin grow. They smiled pleasantly and wished me well in my impending addition.

I swayed out of the building into the late September sun and thanked my friends for their help and guidance. I breathed a sigh of relief as I got into the passenger side of our car and settled in behind the air conditioner vents. I was exhausted, enormous, and emotional. My mind told me differently, but my heart felt as if an entire room full of adults had maliciously attacked my little boy for two hours. They had talked about all the things he couldn't do. They had talked about how different he was, how he didn't do what other kids could, how he lacked empathy and connection, how he couldn't cut with scissors or ride a trike, or how he couldn't bounce a ball, hop, skip, gallop, or stand on one foot. They told me how he couldn't be understood, how limited his speech was, how he couldn't tolerate kids near him, and how difficult he was to redirect. They told me how he had extreme sensitivities to sound, light, textures, and touches. They said he wasn't perfect, and they said it in a hundred ways. I knew that when I got home, all I would want to do was hold him and protect him from the cruelty I had witnessed.

I knew even then that they hadn't meant to be cruel, that they had a plan to help and that they simply needed me to see where he needed it and what they are going to do towards that end. It didn't matter. It hurt. I hadn't really expected that. I felt a great deal of relief, however, that he was going to be allowed to stay with the teacher who was working so well with him. That was a blessing for sure.

I could see the pain I felt reflected in Brett's eyes, too. We were quiet on the way home. We were sad that we had to go through such an ordeal as a family because it felt unfair. It was finished now, and we were relieved to have the meeting behind us. We had another pressing engagement because we were about to add a couple more pitter-pattering feet to our home.

As the next few days softened the harsh words that rang around in my head, I found myself ready for the next step. I was ready to greet Aaron—or I thought I was. I am not sure there was really any way to prepare for Aaron, bless him.

Justin had a big learning curve ahead of him! Besides all of the therapies and constant work we did with him, now we expected him to learn how to be a big brother. Justin wasn't at all sure he appreciated this new interloper. He adjusted slowly to this new little entity and I did my best to stay balanced between the both of them. Aaron rewarded me with the gift of cuddling. That was something Justin didn't tolerate, but Aaron adored. I hadn't realized just how much I needed that. I would come to find so many things Aaron would add to my life that I didn't even know were missing.

Before I knew it, ten months had rolled by. Justin had developed more and more language. He was potty trained. He could scoot, if not pedal, a tricycle. He loved to sit and look at books, and, as I would learn later, was actually reading the words on his own. Pretend play still eluded him, but he began to spend a few minutes in the presence of his peers. He started to argue with me about things, and I realized what a welcome and vital skill that was. He was making progress.

In the meantime, Aaron smiled, turned over, crawled, reached for me, walked, looked for me, talked, cuddled, and climbed. I had promised myself before he was born that I could handle it if he had the same delays, but I was glad he did not. Thankfully it had never crossed my mind that if Aaron had had delays, they could indeed have been much worse than Justin's were.

One morning as Aaron and I dropped Justin off at preschool, the director called me over. He informed me kindly that the district had not been paying Justin's tuition as they had indicated they would at the IEP meeting. I assured him I would check into it directly, and I made several phone calls to the folks who had not only been present at our IEP, but who had been witness to many. *Had I misunderstood? Did I hear something that others had not?* The answer from every angle was, "No" Everyone had met the same conclusion, and the district had suggested that we leave Justin in his current preschool. They had set goals that were to be overseen by his teacher, and the expectation was that the district would fund it because they had not offered any other setting to accomplish the goals they had set.

The immediate response from the district officials was that they were very happy to see Justin flourish but that they had not put it into the contract that they would foot the bill. They suggested that if I desired, he could enroll in their special day class for the kids with developmental disabilities. I have found that districts can be sly and are quite competent to deal with those of us who come to this situation uneducated in the ways of school district bureaucracy and emotionally wrought. But I knew what I had to do, so I called for fair hearing.

For months, I had begun to find my feet and was educating myself. I had formed relationships with the therapists as well as many other moms who were going through similar trials to mine. I had studied the federal laws governing the education system in this matter, and I knew what our rights and the district's were.

I could see how well Justin was doing in his current setting but after learning some of the protocol and under the advisement of an advocate I had retained, I went to observe the special day class. I saw about a dozen kids with varying needs and delays: None had language, none were potty-trained, many had severe behaviors, and one teacher and one aide corralled them all. The speech therapist would come in and work with *all the kids*—a dozen three- or four-year-olds—a couple times a week. It wasn't very productive. I kindly watched and made mental notes.

Before we had our fair hearing, we went to mediation to try to settle the disagreement before a judge has to make the call. With a mediator present, we went forward with the placement discussion in which the big question was where would the district allow Justin to be? I had learned that the law allows for children to be in what is deemed the "least restrictive environment" for learning to take place.

That simply means that he must be placed in the class that allows him to learn with the least amount of restrictions. When the district psychologist asked what my impression had been of the special day class, I found I could hold my tongue no longer. I firmly said I thought they'd be lucky to have him. I went on to explain that he had more skills already than any of the children in the class. He would not benefit or grow because he needed kids to model. He was starting to mimic behavior at his current school, and the behaviors I saw in special day class were not ones he needed to learn. In short, I said this was a very "restrictive environment." They heard my words loud and clear and knew that I knew the letter of the law. The mediators were perplexed that the district had allowed the disagreement to go so far; there really was no question at all as to where Justin belonged because we had asked for so little.

That did it. With one protest, I had made a name for myself as one who would not allow her son to be overlooked, underestimated, or conveniently collated. It would be years before I went to an IEP and was second-guessed. They knew I knew how to play the game. I never asked for, nor did I want Justin to have more than his share of services. I didn't want anything above and beyond; I just wanted what was allowed to ensure his continued growth and achievement. He received well-managed, uninterrupted, and appropriate placement and therapy thereafter, and he thrived.

Chapter Three

Under the Umbrella

The Weathered Path to Acceptance

We all huddled closely under this umbrella of interlocking and overlapping diagnostic characteristics while options, therapies, treatments, diets, advice, appointments, and medications rolled off and puddle at our feet for us to wade through. There was a lot to fathom and many things to try to understand. There were things to accept and learn to not dwell on. There were advisements to mull over, fad diets and unconventional treatments to peruse, appointments to keep, and medications to consider. It often felt like a deluge.

Letting go was a long process. It took a long time to finally realize that the perfect family we thought we'd have wasn't even possible. I barely remember now what I thought perfect was. I know this wasn't it. I never thought I'd end up with an alphabet soup of doctors, therapists, and counselors involved with my kids, my husband, and me.

Autism is what they commonly refer to as a spectrum disorder and falls under the umbrella of Pervasive Developmental Disorder (PDD). PDD encompasses five distinct but related disabilities:

Autism Spectrum Disorders (ASD): As I have previously discussed, the parameters of, PDD—NOS, which stands for Pervasive Developmental Disorder—Not Otherwise Specified, is a diagnosis used when many but not all the characteristics of autism are met. It is also used more often in younger children who might not exhibit some criteria yet to meet the diagnosis of autism, but who display certain characteristics that place them under that umbrella.

Asperger's Syndrome: This is characterized by a lack of social skills, poor coordination and concentration, and a restricted range of interests. A person with Asperger's does not usually have a significant language delay and might often have above-average intelligence. They might have trouble understanding subtleties used in conversation such as irony, sarcasm, and humor. Asperger's syndrome, though originally described in 1944 by Hans Asperger in Vienna, has not been widely used as a diagnosis until the last decade.

Rett's Syndrome: This is diagnosed primarily in girls and seems to allow for typical development for the first six to eighteen months of age, at which point a regression or loss of abilities begins to occur. Gross motor skills regress, followed by an obvious loss in speech, reasoning, and hand use. The repetition of certain meaningless gestures or movements is an important clue in the diagnosis.

Childhood Disintegrative Disorder (CDD): This is a rare condition originally described in 1908 but has only recently been "officially recognized." Children with this disorder develop a condition that resembles autism but only after a relatively prolonged period, usually two to four years, of clearly normal development. Regression in multiple areas of functioning occurs with CDD, usually involving ability to move, bladder and bowel control, and social and language skills. By definition, this is only diagnosed if there have been at least two years of normal development and if the onset occurs before age ten. All of these have a wide spectrum of varying degrees of characteristics and involvement for any given individual.

I started catching on to Justin's delays just before he turned two. I am not sure, but maybe I was a bit slow on the uptake. When Justin was very small, Brett's mom would watch him a couple mornings a week while I went to work. I remember one morning when he was about eighteen months old, she pointed out that Justin didn't look at her when she called his name. She said it was very hard to get his attention, and she was concerned that he didn't speak. Now, being the overprotective, first-time, making-this-up-as-I-go mom that I was, I simply said I hadn't noticed that it was a problem.

I told myself she was wrong. I told myself that she wasn't doing it right. After all, not only didn't I want anything to be wrong, but if there was, I should have been the one to notice first. I pretended he just wasn't interested in her. Of course, in the back of my head, I knew the truth. The truth was, he wasn't—he wasn't really interested in any of us a lot of the time. I just didn't know that wasn't normal. After all I had heard from everyone, "All babies are different," "Girls mature faster than boys," and "He will when he's ready."

While my mother-in-law's comment triggered a protective and assertive instinct in me, Brett was happy to let me follow whatever course I chose to satisfy my concerns. He didn't see any real cause for alarm at this point. He humored me and kind of shrugged off my panic.

So while I was vehemently denying the possibility of any kind of problem, I was also wrestling with what my first move should be to follow up my mother-in-law's assertion a little farther. I called our new pediatrician, a parent's first line of defense. I explained that Justin had started to say a few words several months before, but now the words were gone. I told her that he was very difficult to redirect, and it was hard to get his attention. I told her he didn't respond to his name. Dr. McBratney thought Justin, at eighteen months, was still within his developmental age group. She said that I should keep reading to him to help build his vocabulary and that she would evaluate him in six months when he was two.

We read books like mad—five or six books every night at bedtime and during the day. He loved them. He could point to anything I asked him to find. His favorite was a Winnie-the-Pooh book with all the characters. He loved anything with animals, and he would sit on my lap as long as I would read. He would even look at books without me. He didn't want to be hugged, he didn't want to be rocked, and he didn't want to be confined in a blanket, but he did love to sit and read. I would speak clearly and follow the words and pictures with my finger to show him what I meant. He seemed mesmerized, but it was hard to know how much was really sticking in his mind. I didn't know it yet, but nearly everything we read about stuck tight.

Breakthroughs in development came in towering peaks followed by long and stagnant plateaus. Neither Brett, nor I thought it would be so much work to get to know our son. I remember one evening while Justin and I were home alone at dinner time, he came out to the kitchen to find me. I was cooking, and Justin came to me carrying a huge clear plastic teddy bear that was full of blocks. I turned and crouched down on the floor next to him; both of us had our knees tucked up under our chins. I knew if he sought me out, there must be something special to see. He pointed to the bear and said, "Ah-clew." At first, I didn't know what the excitement was all about, nor did I understand what he was saying, but I smiled knowingly and nodded in agreement. Suddenly, I realized what he meant and air failed to fill my lungs. He was pointing to the bear's paw print that was hardly visible, just a clear stamp in the plastic. My smile was replaced with an astonished stare. The paw print was a "clue," like he'd seen on *Blue's Clues*, his favorite TV show! He had made this great discovery and wanted to share the revelation with me! I remember with tears spilling down my cheeks and my eyes burning, I covered my mouth to stifle my sobs, but my heart soared. Through Justin's seldom extended invitation, I had a window into his world. He was sharing something that he had recognized and was telling me about it! This was a first, and it was gold!

Brett found even fewer of these highlights than I did and felt a bit like an outsider. He wasn't home enough to be present for many of these little exchanges. He tried to get to know Justin, but that was a very hard thing to do if Justin wasn't in the mood because Justin didn't interact willingly ninety-nine percent of the time. My husband had no idea how to relate to Justin, and he felt even more isolated from Justin's world than I did.

By the time Justin's two-year checkup rolled around, he said about twelve words. Typically by this point children should have somewhere around fifty words and be starting to use two- to three-word phrases. Justin was already well behind his peers. Dr. McBratney completed her two-year evaluation and suggested we conduct a hearing test as a place to start. As we left the exam room, I realized I had forgotten to tell her that although Justin couldn't say many words, he could make the noise of any animal you could name. "Does that count as words?" I asked. From her pause and polite smile, I could tell it didn't count.

Justin's hearing evaluation showed a normal range of hearing and did very little else except leave me wondering why it took that horrific, wild-eyed animated chimpanzee hiding behind tinted glass to light up with his symbols to tell me Justin's hearing was normal. Nonetheless, I felt we were one step closer to solving the problem. The audiologist suggested a speech evaluation. I remember thinking, *Well, that won't take long. You can just about count all the words he can say without taking off your shoes.*

Lo and behold, Justin's speech was delayed. (Sorry for the sarcasm, but I seem to have developed a few defense mechanisms over the years.) What I was surprised to hear was that he was at least a year behind, *and* the speech pathologist said he was too easily distracted for speech therapy with her. She suggested I call the Regional Center. *Okay*, I thought, *the regional center of what?* I took the referral and the evaluation back to Dr. McBratney. She agreed that I should call the Regional Center for California and further explained that it was an organization that specialized in state-funded developmental evaluations for children ages birth to three years old and offered placement if he were to need speech therapy. She told me the Regional Center was involved with all levels and ages of disability but focused sharply on early intervention for children under the age of three with the hope of making as much progress as possible in the very formidable early years.

At the same office visit, Dr. McBratney wrote out a referral to also see a pediatric neurologist and a geneticist to rule out several other things, which stung as an insult. Never in my life did I expect that I would be taking my toddler to a neurologist; I never had a reason to wonder if there even *were* geneticists who work with children. From the minute Dr. McBratney handed me the referral, I felt sick. I actually became nauseous. *Why does she think Justin needs all of this? In this day and age insurance companies don't pay for anything unwarranted, but it seems like she knows they will cover these tests. Why can't she just tell me he is fine and I am worrying too much? That's what everyone else does.*

The tests were awful. Having to hold Justin down so that they could take blood from his veins to determine if he had a degenerative genetic disorder was probably one of the worst days of my life. Or maybe it was the next four days as we waited for the results to come back. When the results were in, we learned that there were no chromosomal abnormalities, which was at least a relief. That was one more possibility that we could rule out.

Actually, as the search for a reason continued and I saw little progress with Justin's development, I learned to tune out the well-wishers who tried to console me by telling me that they were sure he was fine. The only thing worse than admitting there was a concern was hearing others pretend there wasn't one. We would sit in office after office, and Justin would struggle through being asked to do things that he couldn't do. There would be tantrum after tantrum as we would leave the offices of some very nice people who I hoped I'd never have to see again.

The process did bring Justin and me closer together as I began to understand him more. There was nothing better than when I saw the wheels turning in his mind and watched him work something out for himself.

As I learned more about Justin, Brett was struggling to understand—and neither of us realized what a toll this was taking on our relationship. I tried to help Brett understand Justin better because I attended every appointment alone or later accompanied by Aaron while Brett was at work or trying to get a few hours of sleep. He often would try to meet me at appointments when he could, and when he couldn't I would fill him in with the details over the phone before I went to bed. I knew he loved his son, but Brett had a very hard time accepting that Justin was struggling so much. He didn't know how to fix it, didn't have a schedule that permitted him to accompany us much of the time, and slowly started feeling all too peripheral.

Part of me felt like it was solely my responsibility as the boys' mother to attend to every need—and there were many—but the other part of me grew weary and resentful from the strain of trying to do most of it alone. I would try to explain the day's events, the doctor's recommendations, and the different therapies and their purposes, but talking to Brett in those late-night hours was like trying to have a chat with the cat—no matter how clearly I spoke, he just couldn't understand. While he worked, he barely heard what I told him each night, and what he did hear me say didn't make much sense to him because he hadn't been there. Likewise, he didn't have much to tell me that I could relate to either. Our lives followed different beats, and the two of us were not harmonizing very well.

But we had to push on. By two and a half Justin had started speech therapy and occupational therapy twice a week and went to preschool three times a week. These things should have been fun, and eventually became so, but in the beginning and for some time to follow, they were quite challenging for Justin. And for me. Justin's formal assessment and diagnosis was done a few months before his third birthday. The diagnosis meant he was eligible to receive services through the state and later through the school district. So while he struggled through pre-school, and I struggled to remember that I was no long thinner if I turned sideways to squeeze past something, I went to work for a few hours and blissfully put the chaos aside for a little while every day. My work was my place of sanity.

After the downpour of assessments and evaluations, the last of the reports trickled in, and Justin's disabilities and delays placed him under the umbrella of pervasive developmental disorder. His actual diagnosis was pervasive developmental disorder—not otherwise specified. It's one of those diagnoses that allows for services without completely dashing a mother's dreams for her child. At two and a half years old they were hesitant to call him autistic, but by age eight, they were not.

The diagnosis hurt, and it takes quite a while for something like that diagnosis to hurt less. It takes desperate phone calls to the therapists and case workers, imploring them to tell you Justin will grow up to get married and live a successful life even though you already know that no one can tell you that. It takes hours of conversations with trusted friends. It takes long walks, silent prayers, and raging tears. It takes an evolution of anger, fear, frustration, pity, sadness, acceptance, and finally admiration. But hope—hope is too elusive just yet. It's much safer to live in the moment and save your dreams for later. For the time being, I gave up some of my unalienable rights of dreaming about my son's future, and I focused on the baby steps. It was much too impossible to imagine the next year, let alone the next twenty. I decided I would wait to see what Justin's dreams were for himself.

In the meantime, I focused on getting Justin the help he needed. The occupational therapists put Justin through the paces over and over week after week. If Justin didn't like something, they only worked harder at it. For example, Justin had tactile sensitivities, so they worked with him on painting mirrors with shaving cream. He hated it but slowly learned to tolerate it better. Other sensitivities manifested in the way he walked, and over time I watched him learn to walk on the soles of his feet instead of just on his toes. Justin couldn't organize his actions well enough to give much reason behind the activities he chose. He often looked like he came into a room and forgot why he was there—only the pattern repeated over and over as he moved from one thing to the next. I watched the therapists put him on all different kinds of swings, which according to research can cause the mind and body to respond repetitively and eventually rewire the mind in an organized fashion. Other theories correlate this swinging to speech development. I watched Justin learn to jump forward. I watched him tolerate other children who played close by. I watched his balance and his posture improve. For example, there was a brief stint when he was two where he looked "older" to me, and after a little while I realized it was because he had started to close his mouth. Prior to that he had never held his mouth closed for any length of time.

At one point, when Justin was four, our neurologist suggested trying Justin on medication to see if we could get him to attend to a task for longer than a split second. His theory was that if he could focus on his therapy better, he might get more out of it. He might learn to talk sooner. As we had been trying a variety of therapy with little success for at least a year at this point, I was open to trying it out even though I was extremely cautious. Although I knew many mothers who were starting to look at drastic and experimental treatments, I wasn't someone to try untested and unapproved treatments on my son, but I was hopeful that well-managed medication would work to encourage his language skills and reduce his anxiety.

The first prescription was an awful experience. I wouldn't have thought that things could get any worse. But I was mistaken. They could and they did. The doctor had prescribed a stimulant, and I was scraping my son off the ceiling—or at least I was drying the water from it after nearly every drop of his bath ended up on the floor, the walls, and the ceiling. He spun through the day with unmatched tension and vigor. He had meltdowns and/or dragged-out tantrums at every transition in the day. He was wired, and I couldn't hold it together any longer. I was in tears when the doctor finally returned my call at 10:00 PM and told me to stop the medication. (Ummm, duh!!)

I was terrified to try again. Justin had morphed into someone I didn't recognize for twenty-four hours, and the thought of trying something else just about paralyzed me. However, I figured we had started down this path, so we needed to try again. The second prescription was undeniably the single most effective thing we had tried to that point. I remember at one point considering seeking out the person responsible for the invention of this most wondrous little tablet that was a godsend. It was a tricyclic antidepressant used for anxiety commonly used in children who exhibit bed-wetting problems. Although I wasn't excited about having to put such a young child on medication, the difference was monumental. I hadn't realized just how much anxiety had crept in to our home and that I was in a perpetual state of tension until after a few days I felt myself exhale and that solid pit below my diaphragm just dissipated and a huge wave of relief spread over me. For the first time in a long time, I smiled. Justin wasn't sleepy or zoned out; he was just collected. He could attend to therapy, he could sit for a while and play, and he could respond to questions or directions. He was happy. He was content. I was ecstatic.

I recognized so many things that I hadn't even realized were a problem, and Justin would continue to work on these things for many years to come through a variety of different mediums.

Justin had met his physical milestones as he grew, but even though the ability was there, the quality of movement wasn't. He always looked unsteady, he was perpetually clumsy, and he drooled nonstop. His muscles pervasively lacked tone, which affected his overall ability of movement and precision and his facial muscles.

The days pounded by, and in time I watched the differences materialize in the boys' development. Things that had come so slowly for Justin seemed to lie before Aaron like a gift. By the time Aaron was ten months old, he was a very capable walker. By the time he was a year old, he had many single words, and by eighteen months he was talking in ever-lengthening sentences. What a blessing that was. At age two he climbed out of his crib and fell onto the little table beside it, sending us on his first trip to the emergency room. There is still a little scar under his nose. At three he baffled the preschool teacher, who seemed at a loss as to how to keep him from buzzing around the room. Aaron's preschool didn't have a chapter in their guidelines that helped their teachers with Aaron, so we decided to move on. At four years old, he challenged the preschool teachers at yet another establishment. We felt we should encourage professional growth in *all* the city's preschool teachers and he checked the staff's ability to respond in case of a pint-size natural disaster. In Southern California, the ability to quickly and effectively get out of the way of falling objects can be a very useful skill to have. I suggested they implement him as part of their earthquake preparedness plan, but they were not amused.

Aaron was certainly full of life and nearly impossible for anyone more than ten years old to keep up with. He brought artwork home that looked like he had created it by rolling himself along the full length of the paper. It was beautiful, and I could certainly tell he had put a lot of himself into its creation. He loved to get messy. He craved movement and tactile play; he loved to crash into things—inanimate or otherwise. We had several meetings with the teachers. It seemed the other kids didn't like being the class's bowling pins or painting canvases. You know no one understands fine art these days.

I hadn't really made too many acquaintances with the other parents at the preschool, and I had little hope of doing so now. If I had made a few friends, it probably would have reduced that everyday feeling that everyone took his or her turn glaring at me from behind Ray Bans. I tried to cheerfully listen to Aaron describe his day while the other parents read over the day's boo-boo reports for their child, courtesy of Aaron. Aaron spent a lot of time listening to me go over the rules with him before, after, and during his day. He felt awful as soon as he saw his actions had hurt one of his friends; he was just so impulsive that he had never had a second to consider what he was about to do. One morning, I prompted him, "Now remember use your …," and he said, "Imagination!" Of course, I was going for "use your words," but how could I argue with that answer?

I had so many conversations with teachers in person and over the phone that I became gun-shy. I always encouraged open communication and wanted to work with the teachers. I wanted to be consistent and respond at home the way the teachers did at school. But some days, because there was nothing else left to do, I tried to move stealthily between the glowers, fasten us all securely in the car, come home, barricade the door, turn the phone off, and pretend everything was normal.

But it wasn't—no matter what training I had. I had already had more studies in early childhood development than many of the teachers had had. I had been through months of behavior management with Justin, which of course spilled over onto Aaron. I had been to seminars and lectures on the subject. I was very good at natural consequences and positive reinforcement. I was very good at being proactive with both boys. It was just that collectively they were better at outwitting me and the rest of the free world. One child at a time I could handle. It was when I was double-teamed that things went south. Most days left me wanting to pull down the shades by 5:00 PM, crawl into bed by 7:00 PM, and pretend tomorrow would be different. Of course, the only things that changed were the nature of the infractions, not the occurrences of them. Yes, that restful, hopeful prayer I whispered to each of them so often,—"Tomorrow is a new day. Tomorrow you get to start fresh and new"—somehow made me cringe. *What would they do tomorrow?*

One fateful morning Aaron, who was four at the time, drank the coffee that had been waiting patiently for me in the cup holder by the driver's seat. I chatted with my friend outside the car for a few minutes while Aaron bopped around inside like a little jumping bean in a can. *Ping, ping, ping.* He thought it would be funny to finish mom's coffee. A half-cup of Starbuck's French Roast poured down the throat of a four-year-old who didn't weigh much more that forty pounds. I knew at that moment we had most likely just embarked on our next long journey. I drove him to pre-school silently saying a little prayer that his day, and the day of all those he touched, would be fine. I wasn't sure what to hope for actually. I already knew that if he had a bad day we would have pieces to put back together to salvage the day, and if he had a good day, it was likely the result of the caffeine. I wasn't ready for the accidental diagnosis that my second child also had a spectrum disorder. I knew that stimulants can cause kids with ADHD to calm down. And being in our 3rd pre-school with him, I knew he showed clear signs of an attention disorder. And of course, I learned when I picked him up that he had the best day ever!I felt broad sided but almost amused. God really does have a sense of humor. *Why else would he put a child with sensory-overload issues in a house with one who craves creating them?*

It was just the beginning of what would be a very long and tangled path. A little stimulant in Aaron was followed by organization and composure. It was virtually as good as a diagnosis. Stimulants are used in children who are afflicted with attention deficit disorders (ADD). It seems like the last thing you would want to use in a child who is bouncing off the walls, but it works. The most concise explanation I have heard is that the child's mind is in a semi-alert state and the hyperactivity is actually the brain's method of trying to arouse itself. By giving the stimulant you cause the brain to come to the level of alertness in which it can function properly, and the hyperactivity is no longer required and is brought under control. If they don't have the disorder, the stimulant will only hype them up more. Caffeine is, of course, the most readily available stimulant and is often suggested as the first trial when one is considering a medicinal approach. It was not my intent to pursue this course at this time of Aaron's young life, but it certainly gave me a glimpse into things that I was no longer able to deny.

I had long expected that there was a possibility Aaron might share some form of his brother's idiosyncrasies. After all according to the National Institute of Mental Health, a terrifying twenty percent of siblings of a child with autism fall somewhere on the spectrum themselves. His language was excellent, his movements were precise, but his social intricacies were yet to be determined. It wasn't a stretch at all to become aware that some of the diagnostic characteristics that are under the umbrella might befall Aaron as well. After all, he was his brother's brother.

I think any parent can get stuck. I don't think there needs to be a specific delay or difficulty that his or her kids face. The disillusionment is the same. Whether you are a parent plying a two-year-old with a lollipop at Macy's so that you can try on one more outfit or tracing your five-year-old's every move at the park because he *is* going to stumble or misinterpret another kid's actions or *both* (while the other moms sit, calmly able to ignore their children and flip through *Good Housekeeping* while chatting amongst themselves and sipping lattes), none of us is quite where we expected to be. I've learned to give myself permission to think that sometimes life as a parent just sucks and not feel guilty about it. I've learned that none of us is half the parent we thought we would be before we had kids.

So here we go again. Take a deep breath. Look ever onward and ever upward by understanding the circumstances, embracing the challenge, and championing their progress.

Chapter Four

Alphabet Soup

Learning Life's Lessons—an Acquired Taste

A padded room was *literally* just what the doctor ordered—for Justin, not me. At least he hadn't ordered it for me yet. There were huge primary-colored mats and pads and suspended swings of all designs, huge bolsters and balls, inner tubes of all sizes, and plastic swimming pools full of dry rice and beans. There were ramps that sent scooter boards sailing, and mirrors that were dressed in shaving cream of all colors. Bright layers of Lycra climbed all the way up to the rafters. There were enormous beanbags and miles of nylon tunnels. It was like a Gymboree Gym on speed.

At age three, Justin and I went twice a week to this amusement park full of therapists and equipment. At the time I didn't understand what occupational therapy (OT) was or how it was supposed to help, but it sure looked like fun. I spent a lot of time watching Justin ricochet from one obstacle to the next while his therapist tried in vain to help him focus in on one thing or another. I remember warning her immediately that he easily got motion sick. (He once had vomited just riding around the aisles in the grocery store cart. It wasn't a pretty sight.) I figured that tidbit would have led her to avoid spinning him in circles on the tire swing. It was funny how surprised she seemed when he threw up. *Rookie*, I thought. I went out to the car to get him the change of clothes that I always kept on hand for just such occasions.

Another therapy was swinging. I still haven't heard a convincing argument about how it helps rewire the part of the brain involved in speech production, but it seems to be a widely accepted theory. Apparently swinging challenges the vestibular system, thereby requiring the brain to strengthen neurological pathways and in turn encourages language development. Consequently, every one of these late talkers could be seen soaring around the room as often as the therapists could get them on one swing or another. The swings went back and forth, side to side, in circles, and even bounced. (But given the vomiting incident, Justin didn't get to go in circles anymore.)

While Justin was exploring the wonders of the OT clinic and Brett was trying to get more than five hours of sleep, I kept up as best I could. I learned quieting techniques and arousing techniques. Ever tried to brush your child? I don't mean his hair; I mean all of him. I was shown how to use a soft plastic bristle brush to massage his skin and then follow with soft joint compressions to alternate the input his brain was receiving and help reduce sensitivity to certain stimuli. Because he was very poor at recognizing where his body was in any given space, they strapped little lead weights around his ankles and wrists. They occasionally even completed his outfit with a lead-weighted vest. All of these things were supposed to help create stimuli for his brain to respond to, begin to reorganize whatever was askew, and give Justin more awareness of his body in space.

Baby Aaron and I would wait in the waiting room at OT for Justin to finish therapy. Aaron kept me on my toes while I followed him around the small waiting room, exploring every nook and cranny. Luckily the room was set up for siblings and had plenty of things to entertain him. It was in this little waiting room that I met some of the most helpful people I would ever know. They weren't professionals; they weren't necessarily highly educated or anybody special. They were just parents. They were dealing with roughly the same issues. They had experiences to share, and they understood everything I said because it was their reality too. No matter what kind of session Justin had and no matter how he acted when he came out after class, they had seen it all before. There was so much peace in being with people who understood without any explanation. I had struggled at all the Mommy and Me classes when he was little because we never really fit. Now, I felt like we belonged.

This time with some very caring people who were highly educated in my field of need became therapy for me as much as it was for Justin. While he was in OT getting rewired, I was finding my feet again. It was like a support group. It felt very good to know I wasn't alone in what I thought, felt, and dealt with. Twice a week, I sat and visited for nearly an hour with whomever was there. It was ideal.

I needed to be heard, but even more than that I needed to hear other moms and dads talk about what they were going through. I felt much less isolated and much less imperfect. I had tried to keep much of my concern from Brett because it only upset him that he didn't know how to help. I also think he felt cheated because he compared the boys and our way of life to families who seemed to have it all together. (He worked in Hollywood where no one has it all together.) But he saw quiet and engaging little girls and boys who led their teams in scoring, dads with all their toys and free time, and moms who didn't double-knot their shoelaces and hadn't exchanged styling their hair for a ponytail.

In retrospect of course we should have found a way to stay interested and stay plugged in to each other's lives. I just didn't have the energy if he didn't have the interest. It isn't hard to understand why the divorce rate of parents with special needs kids hovers somewhere around the eighty percent mark. There isn't anything left for you to give to anyone else at the end of the day. Brett did go to a few conferences on autism with me, and I always left feeling like we were the luckiest people in the room. The speakers there talked about those individuals with whom they had had the privilege to work. They joked kindly about the idiosyncrasies in these great kids, and I felt so blessed to have a child of my own who was that special and had so much to offer. Brett never felt so enamored. He never really understood the joy I felt, and it made me sad that he couldn't find the beauty in our greatest gifts. Brett and I were still married, but we didn't lead the same life.

There is a lot to learn when you start down this kind of road. One of the first things you learn is that the people who you rely on to have all the answers just don't. Your family wants to take away the discomfort, so they tell you it will all be okay. Your friends want to support you, so they say they understand. The pediatrician wants to feel necessary, so he shows you graphs and charts that your child's growth and development *aren't* on. None of this helps. None of it brings answers, and all of it leaves you swimming alone among terms you don't know, prospects you can't fathom, and goals you have no idea how to reach. I started to realize that I knew more about Justin's diagnosis than the pediatrician did, more about behavioral management than our parents did, and more about developmental milestones than my friends did. So what do you do when your first line of defense leaves you defenseless? You grow. You read. You go to conferences. You study. You listen. You become your child's strongest advocate and the one who knows him inside and out even if he can't tell you. You become proactive and you figure out what has to happen next.

Justin began collecting this laundry list of therapists when he was two years old. His team included a speech and language pathologist (SLP), an occupational therapist (OT), a behavior therapist, an inclusion counselor, a preschool teacher, an adaptive physical education therapist, a neurologist, a pediatrician, a case worker, and a T-ball coach. We had a solid team, but that didn't stop us from getting the rug pulled out from under us occasionally. Justin saw most of these people on a weekly basis, and some more often and others as needed. He had goals set in writing, and people who helped him achieve them backed Justin up. He needed to learn to talk or at least communicate. He needed to learn to jump, skip, catch a ball, hop, balance, put his clothes on, tolerate cooperative play, pedal a tricycle, pretend, hold a crayon, sit in circle time, and use the toilet. It was obvious by this point that he needed to be taught in a one-to-one setting because he wasn't going to learn by the example the other kids set. He was in his own world and never looked at the other kids. They just didn't exist for him.

By first grade Justin had started to tolerate other kids playing near him and would allow them to join him sometimes. He occasionally wanted to join their games but wasn't sure how to make that happen. Usually that meant he would barge in, grab the ball, lie in the middle of the puzzle, or knock things over. He just had no idea how to ask to be included.

One of my worst fears was that other kids would notice this and tease Justin because he was different. For Justin he barely realized that the kids keeping him from being first in line had a pulse. They were merely objects that caused him stress. I always worried that Justin would notice he didn't do things as well as the other kids, but up until then it hadn't been a problem. But by the middle of first grade, things began to change a bit.

During his IEP that year, his first grade teacher spoke up about a concern. She was really a doll. She adored Justin, and I think it hurt her as much as it did me to have to lay out all the struggles on the table. She brought out a project Justin had worked on. It looked like a lot of torn white construction paper glued on a bigger piece of light blue construction paper. She handed me the artwork and explained that it was to have been a tear art snowman. The kids were supposed to tear the paper into the shapes to create the project, but Justin couldn't do it, which by itself was no surprise. His fine motor skills were quite delayed, and it would have been a very difficult task for him. What had brought this to her special attention was how as he tried to do the work, he watched the *other kids* do their tearing and he started to cry because he said he couldn't do it like they could. He knew theirs was better. He had *never before* looked outside his own world long enough to compare what he could do to what other kids his age could do—until then.

Our personal safety net of sorts, intertwined with the social distance between Justin and his peers, had given way. That gap that we had been trying to bridge had just become a little bit smaller. But with the strides also came the painful personal truth that he wasn't as good at these things as his classmates and he now felt the pain of being different. My heart broke for him. I was so torn. If he could learn to compare actions, then he could learn from his peers, which is how children learn at this age. The prospect carried great promise. The flipside was the crushing realization that he would notice the other kids could all do things he couldn't, and they could do them very easily. I learned this day just how hard it is to help the ones you love and let them feel the sting that comes with growing up, especially when you know you are part of the reason it hurts. You see I had sat in those meetings and asked for the help he needed to make the progress required to catch up and keep up. I asked them to challenge him. I knew it was for his own good, but somehow that only made it worse.

For example, one of the most difficult things for Justin was his speech. He had a tremendous receptive vocabulary, what he understood was phenomenal, but what he could express was minimal and very hard to understand. We spent two hours a week with a speech pathologist and numerous hours in between practicing. Justin needed strong tangible and visual explanations in order for him to understand where and how to adjust his skills, so for one entire summer I painted his lower lip with peanut butter and asked him to scrape it off with his top teeth so he could practice figuring out how to produce "f" sounds. One hot summer day while sitting at the kitchen counter under the air vent, "tirecuk" became "firetuk." It was a huge step. We spent the next months pretending we were the giant from Jack and the Beanstalk …saying Fe, Fi, Fo Fum!

Because I worked so closely with him, I understood Justin's every word, but I knew no one else could. I decided early on that although I could help keep him from getting so frustrated that he would not shut down, I also needed to play dumb for a while to encourage articulation with every sentence he tried. But I felt so mean sometimes. Justin struggled not just with producing sounds and pronouncing words, but also putting sentences together in ways that made sense to the rest of us.

On the other hand although he had difficulty expressing his own mind, he had no trouble reading. He was already quite proficient before he stepped into kindergarten just after turning five. He also had no trouble reciting word for word something he had read or something he had heard on television. He often sounded like a walking advertisement or the world's smallest professor. He had a lot to share, but he just had trouble getting it across and trouble figuring out how his own words should fit together.

No matter what I had come to expect, I never ceased to be amazed. Once when Justin was six and Aaron three, the four of us were out looking at Christmas lights and Brett and I were chatting about the lights and the decorations. Justin, as he often is, was in his own little happy place and Aaron was babbling happily about the pretty Christmas lights and Santa Clauses on all the lawns. Justin piped up from his booster chair in the back seat and started describing and giving examples of symbiosis. This would be the cohabitation of two organisms that live together in a mutually beneficial relationship. The example Justin used was the beneficial bacteria that live inside tubeworms at the bottom of the ocean because both benefit from the relationship. I was tickled, and Brett was floored. I took a couple minutes to explain to Brett what Justin was saying. "How does *he* know that?" he asked. I explained to him that what goes in to Justin's mind stays locked in tight for future use.

Listening to Justin was a lot like listening to a tiny adult, except he was very hard to understand. He always spoke on topics beyond his years and used language he adopted from the sources he cited, which made him sound strangely like the world's youngest expert.

On another day later that year, I was listening to one of Justin's "lectures", this one on the eating habits of certain dinosaurs. He was explaining the difference between carnivores and herbivores to me. Using my window of opportunity to interact with him on his topic of choice, and since I was busy making steaks for dinner I asked him, "So then, what is a cow?" He didn't miss a beat, his little eyes flashed and he said, "*Oh,* a cow is an *ungulate.*" I had heard the word *ungulate* in some past zoology class, but I really couldn't recall what it meant and I certainly hadn't used the word when addressing my kindergartener. It was one of those moments when I remember where I was, what I was doing, and what time of day it was. I have never been so proud and confused in my whole life. I stopped and stared dumbly at him for a moment and then I asked him if he really knew what ungulate meant, and he said, "Yeah, it has cloven hooves!" I honestly have no idea where he learned that word—and some of the others he knew. I had provided all the books I could find, and he had read them. To this day, I still don't remember ungulate being in any of the books we had read, but I suppose it must have been.

The boys both offered different things for me. With Justin came unexpected challenges and unbelievable insights. With Aaron came so much of what I hadn't even realized I was missing. Aaron loved to cuddle. He loved to be rocked. He loved to engage me in his games and he loved to get my attention. I couldn't be far from his side at any time and I never worried he was going to wander off. He needed me. That was a wonderful feeling. I probably overdid it rocking him to sleep when he was very little. It was something that Justin hadn't allowed me to do and I relished every moment of it with Aaron. For all the time I spent waiting for Justin to talk, I was rewarded with the words that came flowing effortlessly from Aaron. His big bright green engaging eyes and his wonderful little conversations were like gold. A welcome and long awaited experience.

Justin's social development was still fairly limited compared to the kids in his class. Against my better judgment, I allowed Justin to participate in the kindergarten holiday program at his teacher's request, but the last place he belonged was onstage. He didn't cause any real distraction because they kept him fairly well pinned at the back and flanked by adults, but the curtain swayed and twirled behind the other kids more than it should have. Our great American flag tottered precariously on the edge of the steps on at least one occasion. He didn't sing the songs, and he didn't pretend to participate, but I think he enjoyed the pretty lights. It was hard to watch, and I silently cursed the teacher for putting us all through this production. As Justin descended with the rest of the budding thespians, Aaron wriggled in my lap and beamed at Justin and announced, "Dat's my brudder, Justee." It was a subtle reminder. Oh, how I wished my eyes saw as purely and innocently as Aaron's did that day.

Between the SLPs, OTs, MDs, PhDs, teachers, and aides, Justin had an alphabet soup of team players. He had a lot of homework and a lot of people rooting for him. But we had to remember to find time to be a family and to let Justin just be a kid. We tried to find places to go to have fun, but there were limits. Some places are just better to avoid at certain times in life. We avoided parks, birthday parties, playgroups, and water parks as best we could because there were always too many opportunities for things to go wrong. Justin didn't share his space or his things at all, and he didn't have any qualms about unseating an innocent toddler if he felt it was his turn to swing. He had no problem helping unprepared urchins down the slide if they took too long to situate themselves, and if all else failed, he would venture far away from everyone without a care in the world. Birthday parties offered visually over stimulating colors and decorations; loud, bouncy music; squealing kids high on punch and cupcakes who seemed to bounce off the walls; and gifts that were off limits unless you were the guest of honor. These little interludes were always good for an automatic breakdown, and we were sure to run into situations that none of us knew how to handle because he wasn't very good at interacting yet. Controlled environments were better playgroups. And then we always avoided water parks. I never understood what would possess someone to design a kids' cove where parents watch helplessly as their offspring scale a ladder up the side of a watery volcano only to disappear over the back side as they slip down one of four slides that lead to different twelve-inch deep pools? Was I the only one who thought that was a bad idea? We lost Justin more than once at a water park. It is very difficult to see through water spraying up out of the ground and hard to move fast enough around wet little kids while you sort through them looking for your own. I would help Justin and Aaron up the stairs on the side of the volcano and then make a mad dash around to the other side and try to reach them in time to see them slip down the slides. Though it was impossible to guess which slide they would chose and I could almost bet that they would pick different ones, leaving me to decide which one to collect first. Do I grab the kid who is still pretty little for the depth of the pool, or the one that will bolt as soon as his feet hit the deck for whatever catches his eye? Days like this left me wondering, "what was I thinking coming here?"

Pizza places with giant rodents are always fun too! I don't think that I was always so nervous in places of chaos. I think it was a learned reaction. All the other mommies took their kids to play at these indoor play centers that served cardboard pizza and offered a variety of games and things to play on, so I took my boys too. Aaron did well enough, though I don't think anyone leaves there without feeling somewhat shell shocked. We always had some calming down and repair work to do when we were done. Aaron never strayed too far away. He played well in the company of other little kids and seemed to know his limits. He would come and check on me and make sure I was within sight. Justin, however, would venture into the tubes of the hamster trail maze suspended from the ceiling and wriggle through the labyrinth, all the while climbing over kids and squishing them aside as he made his way in whatever direction he chose. He was a big kid and not much slowed him down, including small bodies of unsuspecting children. I would watch helplessly from the deck while he squeezed and pushed his way through the tubes. I would call to him over the din of the electronic games erupting around me, to no avail. Even if he could have heard my voice, he couldn't tune into it. There were too many distractions and he was usually in his own world. I couldn't reach him. He couldn't hear me, and wouldn't respond, and someone always ended up in tears. We just didn't really belong here either.

We did find some excellent, if unconventional, spots to investigate. While on vacation in Rhode Island when Justin was two, we were exploring an old part of town and wandered onto the grounds of an old white steeple church reminiscent of something in which Paul Revere might have hung a lantern. Tucked back behind it was a wonderful old cemetery. There were tall, intricate headstones bearing worn inscriptions from two hundred years ago and large flat tombs that seemed to rise out of the uneven ground. The small cemetery was fenced, and there was only one gate to allow visitors passage. No one else was there, and for the first time in a very long time I felt my whole body and soul relax as I realized Justin couldn't go too far as long as I guarded the gate. Justin had a perfectly lovely time playing peek-a-boo from behind the tombs. He climbed up and over the tombs, lay down to rest on one while he gazed up at the clouds for a few seconds, then disappeared off the other side, and wound his way through the history around us. For a fleeting moment I thought this might appear disrespectful of those interred and then chose to believe that they might just approve this little blond breath of fresh air pitter-pattering about. Had it not been for this little fenced yard, I might not have even seen the fall colors for which New England is renowned and found it possible to relax on vacation—so long as the only people around were the dearly departed. There can be peace in unexpected places.

Sometimes that is what it takes to combat the feeling of isolation that comes upon me. So when I have been sitting and listening to well-meaning teachers and therapists discuss Justin's progress and the plan for his academic future, I allow myself the time it takes to absorb it all. I am clear about the program. I understand the goals. I will work hard to see that all that can be is accomplished. But then as I leave the room and come out blinking into the daylight, my mind is still abuzz. I feel the warmth of the day, I feel the touch of the breeze, I smell the light fragrance in the air, and I listen to the children playing on the school yard. I consider not so much where we are going but from whence we came. I take time to be in awe of my son and remember the miracles. I realize that at the end of the day, not many of those kids will have worked as hard as Justin did today at whatever it was that he tried to do. I consider their parents and wonder if they find the time to marvel at their children.

I am greeted at home by peanut butter kisses and crumbly hugs. A quick kiss at the door, and Brett leaves for work just as I get home. I put away the paperwork and lesson plans and settle in for the evening of trivia that Justin and Aaron have been waiting to foist on me. Their questions baffle me. I have never been very good at figuring out how genetics works for Pokemon, and I don't understand their evolutionary process. I am ill equipped for this challenge and concede my defeat. But their beaming faces remind me that I am the one who won this round anyway. Tonight, I will partner with Pikachu to battle evil forces, and tomorrow I will figure out how to get the peanut butter out of the carpet.

Justin and the pumpkins! 1996

Aaron and the giant pumpkin! 1999

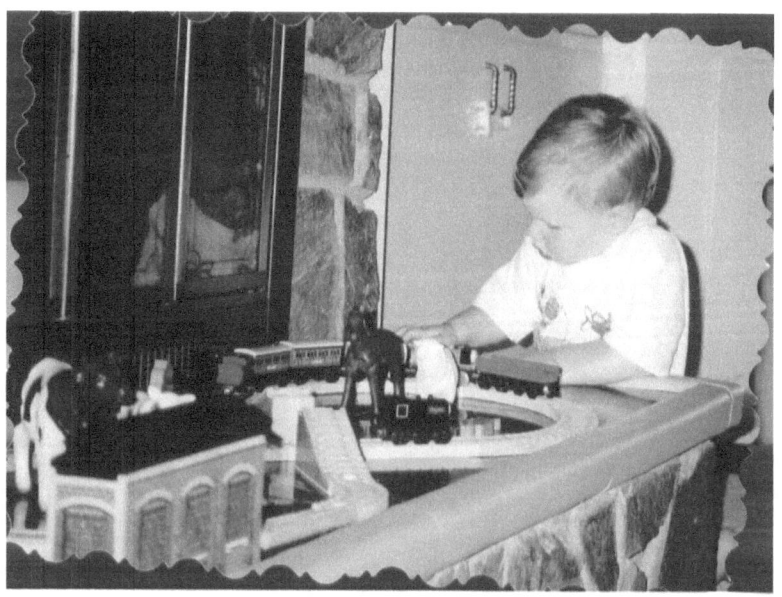

Justin and his beloved Thomas the Tank Engine 1997

Justin at Occupational Therapy climbing the lycra 1998

Justin reads to mom and Aaron. Our evening routine 2000

Young Jedi are ready for Trick or Treating!

Aaron at his finest! 2002

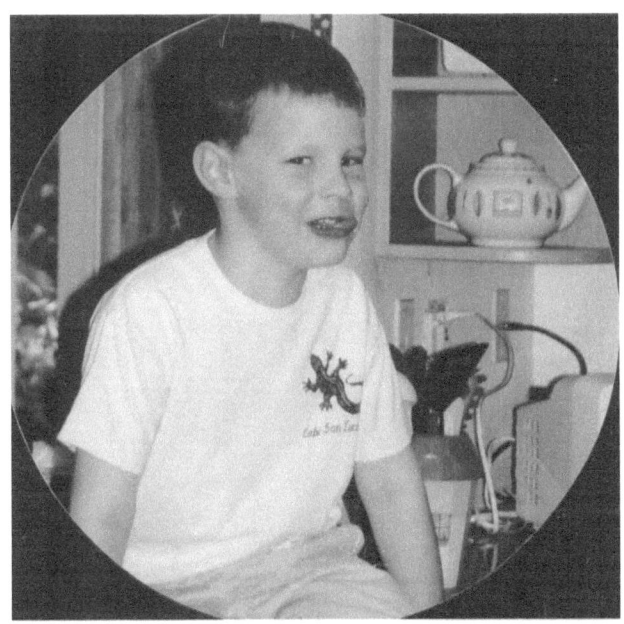

Justin shows his sense of humor! 2002

A friendly game of chess. 2001

Justin Thomas Anderson 2005

Chapter Five

Peanut Butter Fingerprints

The Sticky Path through Disillusionment

Ever tried to get peanut butter out of shag carpet? It's an impossible task. I contemplated the cost of replacing one thousand square feet of carpet because of a six-inch-by-six-inch square of matted nylon fiber that would otherwise be an eternal reminder of the peanut butter and jelly years of life. Somehow the boys managed to effectively decorate the carpet, table glass, portions of the walls, and themselves with the sticky brown concoction. *How did he get peanut butter on the* inside *of his shirt?* I wonder. After working on the carpet for nearly half an hour, I resorted to trimming the worst of it away and leaving the rest to soak for a bit.

I have yet to figure out how these little kids, from the moment they were born, have managed to completely restructure our home. The majority of the walls are still standing, and we haven't had to replace the windows more than once although I did have to scrape paint off of several that Justin had decided to spray paint when he had to "punish" me one day. It astounds me how they have managed to implode the infrastructure of the well-established system of balance and harmony in our home. I know of rebel forces who don't employ such expertise. How do children who are barely tall enough to spit toothpaste into the bathroom sink leave me feeling outwitted on a daily basis? How in a house full of family is it possible to feel so alone and helpless?

When Justin was diagnosed, we began to understand the level of the challenges he faces, some of which I mentioned previously. One big challenge we faced was Justin's inability to pretend, which in turn means he doesn't lie. It is simply too difficult for him to create a story on the spot, and if he does create a lie, he can't adapt it as it unfurls.

Because of this, I have let his teachers know that if they think he might be lying, then they probably have asked the wrong question. For example, I once asked Justin if he had brushed his teeth and he told me "yes!" when I knew he hadn't. I considered his answer and my source for a moment. I reworded my question, "Have you brushed your teeth *this evening?"* He was surprised because he realized what my question really had been. "Oh, no," he replied. Justin had brushed them that morning, and that was what was on his mind when he had answered me the first time. He wasn't lying at all. He just answered the question I had asked. And he was right as always.

Another time I came home from work one afternoon to be greeted at the door by my frustrated husband. Justin had turned six that day and had taken it upon himself to open all of his birthday presents. Brett told me that Justin and Aaron had gone into our bedroom and opened the gifts, which had been set aside for the coming weekend's party. Logically, I figured, it had made sense. He knew it was his birthday after all, and we hadn't told him he had to wait for the party. I never really had to tell him to wait. He wasn't that interested in the first place. If it was out of site, if he couldn't see what it was, it had no appeal. A wrapped present didn't have a lot of draw for him.

As I went in to take stock of the situation, Brett commented further that the boys had snuck in and closed the door before proceeding. "Unh, unh," I said as I turned and grinned at Brett. He was perplexed at my response. I knew Justin wouldn't sneak around to do anything, and he certainly wouldn't close the door. I told Brett that Aaron, our sneaky three-year-old, was behind the whole show. Justin would have felt well within his right to open his presents and would have seen no need to close the door. Aaron, on the other hand, already knew by this age that you shouldn't open a present unless it had been given to you. I could just imagine the little exchange that must have taken place while Aaron convinced his big brother to open his presents. I wish I had witnessed that one!

Even at fifteen years old, Justin still struggles with the challenges he always has had. He still has trouble interpreting social situations. He recognizes this and often studies what confuses him. He has asked me more than a few times what happened in a particular exchange. He still has trouble knowing where his body is in space. His brain just isn't wired clearly that way for him. Often if asked to close his eyes, he will be unable to determine what body part you might be touching.

He has considerable trouble discerning between a toe, a heel, or an elbow when his eyes are shut. Because of these things, he tends to be a bit clumsy. He still has trouble with anxiety and frustration, and he doesn't transition very well from one task to another because he likes predictability. Even transitioning out of school for summer vacation is off-putting for him. It just takes a while for him to work through things even if he will enjoy taking part in the recreation.

Aaron rises to every occasion and supplies endless opportunities for Justin to be challenged and grow. Aaron offers perpetual movement and creates sounds previously thought impossible to replicate. He is impatient and demanding of attention. He expects perfection and demands precision. He won't tolerate redirection and is completely unpredictable. Can you just feel the love? What children could more perfectly set each other off than these two can?

In amidst the turmoil, there are wonderful days on to which I try desperately to hold. When Justin was in fourth grade, he told me, "When I was six, I had a dream that God was in *you,* helping take care of *me.*" That was a good day. I certainly couldn't argue with that. Why else hadn't I already crumbled?

But there are days that no matter what I do to deflect the constant bombardment of frustration, annoyance, and disregard for personal space, the boys seem to find ways around me and to each other's hot buttons. Those are the days I can't wait to get through. On those days, I am faced with questions I can't answer. On those days Justin asks, "What are the rules?" And I give him a short list of the obvious ones: Don't hit; use your words; wait your turn. He corrects me by saying, "Not *those* rules. The *other* ones. The ones the *other kids* know that I don't?" How does one describe the unwritten, unspoken rules that we all inherently understand and take for granted and yet are completely lost on kids like Justin? If someone smiles, how do describe that it might not be because the person is happy. That it might be because they are smug, or deceitful. What about when someone cries with tears of joy, laughs *at* you, instead of *with* you. How do you teach a young child how to tell the difference when it isn't logical and they can't read the cues or fill in the context to match? It can be very frustrating and confusing.

Justin has asked some very difficult questions to answer, the kind of questions that make your heart break and jump out of rhythm. One day when Justin was nine years old, he piped up out of the blue, "What is autism?" It was a good question and one that deserves an honest but careful answer. But it was the first time he ever asked me anything about it. I never kept anything a secret, nor did I speak in whispered tones. Autism is not a bad word in our house, but nonetheless, how do you describe it? My hesitation spurred the next question with a sense of urgency.

"Is it *bad*?"

"*No!*" jumped out of my mouth and was followed by another pause. I said, "Justin, autism is difficult to explain because it is different for everyone who has it. For you, it means you are great at working on the computer and you have a fabulous memory and are excellent at spelling, science, and trivia. It's also why you have trouble writing nicely, speaking clearly, and sometimes understanding people. It is why some things are easier for you than most people and why some things are so difficult. God gave you a very special gift and meant for you to be just who you are."

He seemed content, and I let that settle in. We went on about our day, but he obviously continued to give it thought because an hour later as we were heading out the door, he spoke again.

"Then why do they want to cure it?" he asked.

Damn, that was another good question. I gave it more careful thought.

I asked, "Do you mean like the posters and T-shirts we see that say, 'Cure Autism Now'?"

Justin said, "Yeah."

The only answer that came to me was to tell him, "Because many people are affected differently than you. Some will never speak. Some will never write. Some will never make a friend or have a job. That is why they want to find a cure."

I wanted to be honest, but I wanted him to feel good about himself, too. What a confusing realization for a nine-year-old. I prayed that I had answered him in a way that honored the questions and his own sense of being. I got my answer the next day when his aide wrote a note that said Justin had told her, "God gave me a special brain." That was another good day.

On these exhausting days, the kids take nice long warm baths while I pull all the shades to make night fall a little earlier. Is Daylight Savings still really necessary? Why must it stay light until 9:00 PM? They can tell time now, and they are getting harder to fool. Be careful what you wish for! These things you want them to learn always find a way to bite you back.

For many years I looked forward to what it would be like to re-live the childhood magic of the tooth fairy, of the Easter bunny, and of Santa Claus. I couldn't wait to see those little expectant eyes. Chase little feet back to bed and lie with them listening for sleigh bells. Imagine my surprise when my first born didn't relish those things like I thought all children did. On Christmas Eve, Justin went to bed. He stayed in bed. He fell asleep, and didn't get up until the morning, at which time he made his way to the table and had breakfast. He left his stocking untouched. He didn't check to see if Santa had come. And he didn't care if the cookies had disappeared from the plate. He didn't play the game right! So yes, occasionally I felt a little gypped too!

When Aaron came along, he brought some balance to my long held fantasies of being a mommy. Aaron was just what I had always expected when it came to being a mommy. Aaron let me hold him when he was tiny. He let me hug him when he was sad or sleepy or if we just felt like it. He let me rock him until he fell asleep. He played with me and he upheld my Christmas expectations. Aaron lit up at the promise of Christmas. He was a little disturbed by anyone coming into the house while he slept, even if it was to leave him gifts!

I got to chase Aaron back to bed repeatedly on Christmas Eve (and lots of other nights too, come to think of it!) I got to show him how to look out the window for a glimpse of a tiny sleigh. He couldn't wait to hang his stocking and put out cookies. I caught him sneaking out of bed to try to catch a glimpse of Santa, or at least see if he had come yet. Breakfast on Christmas morning had to wait until after stockings were opened and the chaos of the season was enjoyed to its fullest. Aaron taught Justin how to enjoy the spirit of the day in a way that I had been unable to accomplish. Aaron played the game so well. Justin fulfilled dreams I didn't know I had, and Aaron blessed me with the ones I had wanted for so long.

I wished that Brett could see that we had so many blessings. I wanted him to see the things we had as part of our lives the way that I did. I wanted these little boys, our family to light him up the way they did me. But mostly, it didn't work out that way. Brett and I try to be adults. We try to discuss world events, interests, and upcoming social gatherings, but we can't even get through planning what to have for dinner or what kind of succulents to plant in the garden without some crisis taking place at our feet. I think it must be part of the kid code to interrupt every conversation, important or otherwise. We have managed to find time to go to dinner without them occasionally and even escape for a weekend once every few years, but the day-to-day challenge is relentless. With Brett gone every night, we rarely had time to communicate. We didn't understand each other's lives anymore. When he was home he was glued to the computer. He enjoyed a hobby of timing the stock market in the late years of the 1990's. And his anxiety level and frustration level rose and fell with the market. His interaction with us was largely based on whether or not NASDAQ was having a good day. I didn't have time, energy, or desire to become involved with stocks. I threw some money into Home Depot and Berkshire Hathaway and let it ride.

With the marriage growing progressively more damaged, I felt like I was trying to take care of all of us physically, emotionally, and financially. And Brett just felt like a paycheck. I would challenge that this feeling he had was of his own making. He had a very good job with a very comfortable paycheck, this much is true, but he also has a family that really could use his attendance at some very strategic times. He had a wife that needed him to listen and to help. And sons that needed him to know who they are. Brett began to find more and more comfort in an alternate reality on the internet and managed to never really engage in all that is a necessary part of our everyday lives.

We do try to make time for just us, but it is very hard to find someone willing to watch both boys on a regular basis. We often go out after 8:00, when the boys are both in bed and asleep so that all the sitter has to do is be present in case of some emergency. Very little goes wrong when they are both sound asleep! This means that I am able to relax better and pay closer attention to my date. Unfortunately, by now, I am not even sure I enjoy his company anymore. My hero, the man who is supposed to love me and his family has abandoned us in a lot of ways. He is bitter in his thoughts, and shallow in his actions with us. So we pretend to enjoy our night out. We have a nice meal and smile at one another. We chat about what's going on or what isn't. We hold hands as we head back to the car, but we both know we are heading home, and we will do it all over again tomorrow. The difference is, I don't mind. It's a lot of work but it is my family. Brett just feels short changed. He can't find the beauty. And I don't know what happened to the marriage I thought I had.

The early days of the kids' lives were so much about keeping appointments and helping them strive for things that they couldn't accomplish on their own that somehow between the odd shifts, the constant commotion, the afternoon therapies, and the increasingly complicated behaviors of the kids, Brett and I stopped communicating.

We grew so far apart that we felt awkward on those rare occasions when we were able to get out alone. We felt like strangers. I would have thought, and often expected to feel, that because I was out with my husband so seldom, it would keep everything feeling fresh and new, but instead I mostly just felt lonely and resentful. I often felt as though I ran the whole show. Every day I came home from work, paid the bills, kept the house clean and neat, cooked the meals, did the laundry, ate every meal alone with the kids, and got them bathed and through homework. I packed lunches, gave medications, answered the teachers' communication from the day, and did the dishes. We had stories and bedtime routines every night after we had finished speech therapy, occupational therapy, the social group, T-ball practice, karate, or scout meetings. My refuge from the day was some mindless TV shows, which I relished as soon as the house became quiet, and I had a couple hours to myself before I fell asleep alone and steadied myself to do it all over tomorrow.

We hadn't meant to, but in various ways Brett and I had started to meet our own emotional needs. We turned away from each other and looked to others for support. I knew Brett had no idea what life was like for me or for the kids because he simply wasn't there. It wasn't because he didn't want to be. He didn't have any more time for himself than I did. He worked long and terrible hours. He had a great job that provided ample money, but it did keep him from his family a tremendous amount of the time. I looked to my girlfriends when I needed support. I had other moms and sometimes dads to talk to about things that would come up with the kids. I had found a tremendous support network in my friends, but Brett didn't really even have time to make friends. His hours were so backward from the rest of the world that I think some people wondered if I was truly married.

Brett was never able to come to Back to School Night. He missed Cub Scouts and Vacation Bible School. He missed almost every IEP and parent–teacher conference. He missed T-ball games and school plays. He rarely got to go trick-or-treating with us or even to Friday night festivities that often come up. He even missed things that happened on Saturday mornings because he would have to sleep until 11:00 AM or so. I would end up missing out sometimes, too, simply because it was impossible to attend certain events with both kids. They needed more than I could give them by myself.

Brett always treated the boys lovingly. He called them "Buddy" or "Pal." He would read to them on the weekends. He bonded faster with Aaron but continued to try to forge an ever-stronger relationship with Justin as well. He would try to find ways to reach out to Justin, but he didn't really know his oldest son.

Eventually, Brett began to withdraw from us. The defeat in his mannerisms became more and more evident. He never blamed the boys out loud, but he blamed me.

I didn't have enough time for him if we were out as a family because keeping tabs on Justin and Aaron required constant vigilance. Making sustained eye contact with anyone for very long could prove to be detrimental, and Justin especially was very good at slipping away unnoticed. I also didn't seem to be able to fulfill Brett's needs adequately when we were alone either. Try as I might, I couldn't make him happy, so eventually I got tired of trying. There is only so much disdain a person can take. *Where was my space?* I wondered. *When was it my turn to be attended to?*

Any therapist will tell you that marital relationships will wither if not tended to. All our attention had been ardently and vitally focused elsewhere for quite some time. I'm not sure what we should have or even could have done differently. Even in retrospect, it seems an impossible demand on a family.

Brett was distant from us. We were living in two different worlds, and it seemed to be impossible to mesh them together. He didn't understand the kids and felt disillusioned by their imperfections. He became bitter and resentful. He convinced me that it was my fault that he wasn't happy with what his life had become. He was jealous of the time the kids required of me, and no matter what I tried to do though, it wasn't enough. I had exhausted every weapon in my arsenal. If I wore heels with my lingerie, I was too tall. If I planned a romantic weekend at a nice hotel, I planned to do things in the wrong order because I should have planned "intimacy first, dinner later." It took me many months before I realized I simply couldn't do anymore.

It's not that any of his opinions were wrong, but he was disappointed in me every time. I took it on as my failure. It was a long time before I stopped trying to claim ownership of something that wasn't mine to own. We began to fight when we never had before, and he found solace with someone new.

I had to concede that I hadn't been the perfect wife. How could I have been? There were simply more pressing demands on us as a couple and as parents than anyone we knew. We decided that we needed some space. Brett found an apartment five blocks away and moved out of the house.

This was an impossible situation to explain to the boys, who were eight and a half and five and a half at the time. They had known that we had been arguing for some time, but it was still hopelessly confusing for them and very hard to explain. Brett and I had been married for twelve years, and all the band-aid fixes wouldn't hold up any longer under the sustained strain of the unrelenting realities that we faced every day. But that is a lot for a kid to comprehend, and we hoped they didn't. How do you tell them just enough so they understand why it's necessary and still preserve the relationships and security for them? It was the hardest place that Brett and I had walked through, but it was vital for us to grow if we were to survive. It's easy for us to blame each other, the safe person in your life, for all the bad things you can't control. It's much too easy to act out, and we did much too much of that. We needed time to heal. The things we had to contend with, the everyday trials were the kinds of things many people don't survive. It would have been easier to walk away, but thankfully, I'm not very good at that.

Suddenly, things were different. The nights that the boys would stay with their dad the house was restless. There isn't a house as empty as one where children are absent. The dinner table missed the antics and wayward crumbs. The unruffled beds seemed unnatural, and there were no little wet footprints trailing away from the bathtub. Their bedtime at 8:00 PM came and went, and the walls seemed to automatically echo, "Go back to bed!"—but there was no one there to ignore the request. I knew I could run an errand, get a cup of coffee, or go visit a friend, but I didn't. I stayed home most nights just to keep the house company because the walls needed someone to protect and comfort. And I needed comfort.

Brett and I gave each other physical space, but as parents, we spent more time together than we had in years. We took the care not to call each other because we thought we should and instead started finding ways to include each other because we wanted to. He wasn't going to be there unless I wanted him to be, and he wouldn't come around unless he wanted to. And he always wanted to. The boys and I went to museums and shows, places we had never gone, and we extended the invitation to Brett most days.

We made no demands on each other, and he started asking to do more with the boys. He wanted to know his children better. He made time for each of them individually and also with both at once. He even coached a soccer team for Justin that was made up of all varieties of special needs kids. They began to bond in ways they had never been able to before. I sat back for the first time in almost a decade and just watched—what a vision.

The boys and I planned a low-cost summer of visiting local museums and tide pools. We took hiking trips and picnics, and continued to invite Brett. The wounds slowly began to heal. I watched as Brett grew his relationship with the boys, and of course, that held my interest faster than any advance he could have made toward me. There was nothing more endearing than a man who enjoys your children, especially if you are married to him.

I made no promise as to what I wanted to see happen, but what I witnessed was such a growth in character for us both like I had never known. Slowly over time our wounded hearts mended, broken spirits were renewed, and conviction was restored. I allowed myself the time I needed to feel everything I needed to feel, to own everything that was mine, and to not try to control the things I couldn't. A lot of work and time went into repairing our family, and when the foundation was strong enough, we began to build a life and relationship more secure than it had ever been before. My only request was that Brett would continue to go to counseling, and I did the same for myself. We needed to grow and heal ourselves before we could expect to do it together.

Six months elapsed, and I felt cautiously optimistic that asking Brett to move back in might pan out. One weekend in early September, Brett moved back in, and we embarked once again into the great unknown. We were more united than we had ever been.

So the idyllic ties of matrimony and the undying bonds of parenthood trip us up, gag us, and render us unable to move with purpose or with any sort of composure.

Marriage and family aren't what any of us previously thought. It's imperfect, it's messy, and it's definitely not effortless. It was a lot like the peanut butter that clung desperately to the fibers in the carpet. It was full of bumps, impossible to experience without getting sticky, and a lot of work to enjoy it.

What do you do with the realization that things aren't what you promised yourself they would be? What do you do when you realize that the teeth that the kids haven't knocked out will require major orthodontic intervention from years of an inserted thumb, the peaceful vacation to British Columbia is disrupted by an ambulance tour to Children's Hospital following a headfirst encounter with a park bench, and the person on whom you depend most sometimes isn't brave enough to get out of bed? The divorce rate and number of broken families are testaments to what the general response is to the disillusionment we all face. It becomes a choice. Do we continue to see these things as obstacles to overcome or see them as opportunities for a richer life? Do we turn our heads in the hopes that when we look back things will be better? Sometimes perhaps we do. Or do we grab the camera and try to capture the seconds that become our lives in hopes of preserving some of the fleeting moments?

I remember slowly becoming aware that everything I thought I knew growing up was false. Life wasn't at all like what it had appeared to be. Dads didn't come home to dinner every night, the only reward for a clean house was less dirt, and the kids were rarely tucked neatly into bed by 8:00 PM.

Sometimes it seems impossible. Sometimes I still get stuck in the expectations. Things fly at me from every angle all the time. I am just getting faster at catching the things the first time around and ducking when I'm blindsided. My peripheral vision has become quite adept. It's certainly a necessary skill to hone. It's hard to acknowledge something that causes discomfort or pain. It's hard to want to accept it. That was the first step though, with Justin, Aaron, Brett, and even me.

I can name any number of times when it would have been easier to give in: to stop going to occupational therapy, speech therapy, social groups, Cub Scouts, and doctors; to get a divorce; or to just agree to whatever the school district thought the kids needed without asking questions or requiring more of them and my kids. It takes a lot of work for the boys to manage themselves in a group of people, strangers or otherwise. Everything we do is a lesson or trial. Every situation creates an opportunity to grow. Success isn't achieved in front of the television or the Game Cube although there is always room for some downtime. It takes constant involvement, a lifetime of balance, and focus.

There are easier roads to take than the ones I have chosen, but that's just it. It's a choice. Every time I put puzzle pieces together enough to understand how Justin's mind works; every time I witnessed progress in the boys: a first long-awaited sentence from Justin, a flash of brilliant glee from Aaron, and the glimmer of the man Brett wanted to become; and every time I witnessed the miracles that make up my family, I made the choice to strive for more. I want to witness every accomplishment, and I want to know what it took to get there.

It's a choice to move forward and to not stay stuck. It's a choice to ask, "What do I need to know, and how do I plug in?" It's a choice to look at the things before me and not see pervasive delays but the opportunity to grow with my children. It's a choice to see the potential for great beginnings in my husband when he comes to me broken and defeated. The greatest challenges are really the greatest provision for our own personal growth and fulfillment. How then can we stay stagnant? I imagine what I would have missed if had chosen the easier paths, and what a shame that would have been. With each choice and realization the carpet comes clean—one strand a time. The peanut oil is washed away, and the fibers begin to resemble their original color.

Back in my house after my cleaning attempt, I stared at that small section of carpet because it was now the cleanest spot in the room. (It always seems to be the way, doesn't it? The part you pay close attention to might shine, but that only highlights the other grime around you. It's ironic, really.) After closer inspection I was satisfied that no more debris remained. I folded the paper towels into a thick pad and placed them on top of the wet spot. The heaviest thing around was the toy box (of course), and I put that to rest on top of the towels to absorb the moisture. Hopefully, all that would remain was the halo of clean in the middle of the carpet and the slight fragrance *eau de peanut*.

So the dog got a new favorite spot on the rug, which she washes with vigor; the table was scraped clean, and the kid's clothes were spinning in the washer. Hands and faces only showed the smallest inference of what lunch had to offer, and once again we had moved through one of life's sticky situations. And like so many other times, the clean spots left evidence of the attention that was due to the world around it. But now it was time to move on. I had another task at hand and was trying not to notice the clock at the far end of the room, which threatened that another meal was fast approaching.

It is an ongoing waltz—1-2-3, 1-2-3—and somehow if I can keep in step at least most of the time, the end result might still be ill refined but will at least hopefully be a socially acceptable display of fortitude and proficiency. My children will go into the world equipped with the steps they need to know to do the dance that society demands. I will watch them and enjoy the flubs and the disharmony as they grow, but I have to admit that if I could find a switch to get all my men headed down the right track, I'd be very tempted to throw it.

After the peanut butter incident, I settled down with a cup of tea for just a couple of minutes to regroup. I allowed myself a few delicious minutes to reflect on things that don't matter. How precious and coveted it was to flip through a pointless Hollywood magazine for just a fleeting moment, admiring dresses and feigning astonishment at the celeb goings-on. And as I did, I spied one last wayward peanut butter fingerprint delicately placed just behind the curtain as if it had hoped to hide there for just a while longer. I smiled at its clever refuge and realized that before long there will be no more fingerprints that try to elude me. Maybe I will let that one hide there for just a little while longer.

Chapter Six

Looking for the Light Switch

Fumbling for the Power to Forgive

I have looked. I have folded ears back, spread toes, and spiraled through cowlicks, but there just doesn't seem to be one. Neither of them seems to have a switch. There is nothing to flip, nothing to turn or slide, and no way to tune them in, turn them on, or shut them off. I realize it seems like an odd thing to consider, but sometimes it seems like there's a wire loose somewhere in my kids. I often think I must have forgotten something important at their births. Did we leave something out?

For example, when Justin was in the fourth grade, I would pull up to the curb and park to wait for him to get out of school. As the bell rang, the kids would stream out of the school like a flash flood. Before long, I would see my nine-year-old's reflection in my rearview mirror. He would climb into the backseat of my car and buckle himself in. One day, he forgot to close the door. I reminded him but he didn't respond. Now, we were the only two people in the car, the radio was off, and the engine wasn't running, but he didn't hear me. I knew he wasn't ignoring me. He was too deeply immersed in himself and was somewhere else—present in body but not in mind. I got out, went around, and peered into the backseat. He looked at me, and I reminded him that he forgot to close the door. He jumped as if startled to see me and said, "Oh!" He closed the door so quickly that I had to jump out of the way to avoid it. He hadn't realized that I was still in the door's path, and apologized.

On the way home I ventured another query.

"How was lunch?" I asked. Justin didn't look at me. I decided to try the question with his name to see if I could get a response. "Justin, how was lunch?" I knew to keep it simple on these days.

"What?"

"Lunch? How was lunch?"

"Huh, what?"

"How… was… lunch?"

I got no reply. The inquest went on for a few blocks.

Finally he said, "Fine."

Dare I ask what he had? I thought. *I don't think I will just now. I don't think I could handle it. He has math homework that won't get done, spelling words that won't turn into sentences, and a project that won't be completed. It's not a good idea today. It won't happen. He just isn't with me. He's in his own world today, and I'm not invited.*

Exchanges like this have led to endless hours beating myself up and blaming myself for things in life that I have no control over. Eventually I end up looking for reasons why my children, and Brett and I along with them, are challenged, and the what-if thoughts sneak in. I have wondered if working with X-rays before I was pregnant caused damage to my body, if the doctor's use of the vacuum during delivery was a mistake, or if the few seconds it took Justin to pink up after birth were too long. Sometimes I wonder if I did something so wrong in my life that karma caught up with me. I have even thought if I had gotten pregnant on a different day, then that baby would not have been born with these challenges. But then it hits me: He would not be my Justin, or he would not be my Aaron. And that would never do. I also have to remember that I had no control over these things in the first place.

It has taken a long time to be able to forgive myself, even though I really had not done anything wrong. I believe moms especially try to take ownership of things that they can't control. The truth is I didn't cause any of the circumstances that plague my children. Plenty of veterinarians and their technicians have perfectly typical kids all the time. While I was pregnant, I ate quite well, got plenty of exercise, and even did a maternity aerobics class. But still, being able to forgive myself even though it was beyond my control, is a hard thing to do.

It really is ironic. If someone were to ask me, I know there is nothing to forgive. I love my children just how they are. They are perfect in my eyes and are just how God intended them to be. In fact, I consider it a great honor to be raising two such intelligent and challenging kids. Doesn't it speak volumes that the good Lord has entrusted me with such expectation? I hope so.

There are blessings in the midst of the challenges. Justin can be engaging, friendly, bright, and social. For example, he loves to try to trip me up on any trivia fact he knows. When he occasionally lifts his green-eyed gaze to mine, I know I am blessed. The rarity only makes it mean more. Justin has no trouble keeping up with his classmates most of the time, and he has been known to set the curve on a science test and often has answers even when no one else does. Once, I tried to play an April Fools' joke on him. I burst into his room and exclaimed I had seen an elephant outside. He casually looked up.

"Wrong, they are only in Africa and Asia."

I thought for a second and said, "Maybe he escaped from the zoo?"

He grinned and said, "Not likely."

Foiled by his memory again. He had my number all right.

Justin has a knack for animal facts, spelling, and history. He loves to give bold oral presentations.

When Justin is at his best, he wants to understand those around him. He can tell what the kids mean when they talk to each other, he knows he has to check in with me before going off somewhere, and his speech is clearer. But these social encounters trip him up the most, so Justin has an aide at school to help him read body language, understand sarcasm, decode face expressions, and explain all the little idiosyncrasies that take place on the playground leave him at a loss. For example, Justin has been taught stealing is wrong, but then a kid takes the basketball away from him in a game. Those dueling thoughts can ruin his whole day while he tries to figure it out. And sometimes it only takes one little thing to turn a good day into a bad one.

In some ways, the good days make the other days seem worse because I know what is locked away inside him and I miss him desperately. When it disappears and when he goes back inside himself, it can be unbearable. He can divide fractions, but when I lose him, he can't add single digits. He can spell complex multiple-syllabic words, but on the bad days, he can't spell anything with more than three letters without mixing them up. We can spend days and weeks in frustration and defeat. I know it isn't a choice he makes; it's just how he's wired. Thankfully as he grows older, these episodes are few and far between. But just when I think we might never go back to this desert, we are again stumbling around in the sand, trying to find our way back and stop at any little oasis of communication we can find.

And, yes, I again start looking for that switch.

While my friends marvel at their own children—"She's five years old already," or "I can't believe he's eight"—I gather myself and dig into whatever stamina I have left. I let out an exhaustive breath and pray out loud, "Dear God, Justin's only six."

Aaron tips the scale the other way. He's a kinetic force that stays wound up even when you try to turn him off. He doesn't miss a beat. He rarely fades or hesitates for long. At dinner, he circles the table like an aviator practicing touch-and-go landings on the flight deck and only stops by temporarily for a bite before he is off again. I don't think he's ever made it through an entire meal seated at the table.

I have learned that by giving Aaron his medication before he ever lifts his head off of the pillow in the morning, I can avoid at least thirty minutes of unstructured chaos, tears, and the unwelcome understanding of why some animals eat their young. If I can manage to get to him before the day begins and that first mood-altering adrenaline rush, then we can usually get through breakfast and getting dressed and be out to door in time for school. If not, I have had to unceremoniously pry the flailing noncompliant six-year-old from the confines of my car and deposit him at school still clad in his pajamas. That was a rough morning and not a great afternoon either.

In the evenings I try various ways to help Aaron unwind and relax. We start early enough to allow for playtime in the watery worlds of the bathtub. We rescue various Lego creations from their descent down the drain. We get through teeth brushing and find comfy pajamas, and we apply calming lavender rubs before we settle down to read stories for at least a half an hour. We have one last trip to the bathroom, we make sure the glass of water is half full next to the bed, and then I turn the lights down low. Justin will whisper good night, his voice trails off, and he is fast asleep almost as soon as I close the door. Aaron delights in going to bed. He will climb into bed and snuggle down, but then he will get up. By 8:15 PM he is tucked a second time. The pattern continues at 8:30 PM, 8:46 PM, 9:13 PM, 9:34 PM, and 10:07 PM.

He doesn't have a switch either. God knows I have looked for that.

I spent an entire summer sitting in silence in the hall outside his bedroom door while I waited for him to fall asleep, a tactic devised to keep him in his bed instead of coming to look for me. It has the added benefit of catching up on all those novels I had been meaning to read. I enjoy curling up with a good book, unless it is on an unforgiving floor as pictures of babies long grown up and relatives long passed stare down at you. How is it possible to feel that a photograph is criticizing you? I know, I know *"In my day we wouldn't have made such a fuss...In my day children were seen, but not heard...in my day children went to bed when they were told and stayed there"*...I doubt all of that! What do they know? The biggest thing they have to worry about now is keeping their frames balanced on that little nail while hoping the swords and hockey sticks don't swing too wide as they pass down the corridor. Who asked them anyway?

Just having children brings out a lot of interesting new and previously untested ingredients to the soup. Having children with special needs just salts the pot and causes a lot of self-reflection and re-working of the recipe for success. It can be difficult at times to see the beauty of the spilled milk on the table that is slowly seeping under the glass top and dripping onto the chair upholstery, the muddy footprints that tattle the passing of a tiny foot soldier over the newly washed Pergo, the puddle-stricken tile doused by a giant tsunami that even the porcelain sea wall can't contain, or the ear-splitting, blood-freezing crash from the other side of the house where two calm boys sat only moments before.

What if that spill is the result of a little boy who just tried to pour his own milk on his cereal for the first time? Forget the disturbance for a moment and imagine the little boy poised over his bowl with a jug that weighs as much as he does. He furrows his brow as he carefully aims, and the milk spills slowly at first into the Rice Krispies, but the torrent overcomes him, and the wave rolls up the side of the bowl, taking most of its contents with it. This wasn't a disaster; this was a perfect storm. There is more here than the splattered table; there is accomplishment, pride, ownership, and fruition.

Perhaps the little muddy footprints don't tell about a naughty child but of a marvelous adventure. Perhaps this was the fierce journey of a great explorer, an able pirate, or a young wizard. The footprints don't lead across the kitchen floor and fade down the hall; they lead masterfully through a child's imagination. They hold untold wonders of a world that we are regrettably too old to fully enjoy anymore. They are the remnants of a marvelous tale where the hero always prevails. He is in desperate need of a bath now, but just moments ago, he saved the world from certain demise.

I help our conquering hero, Aaron, slip into the tub and watch the bubbles swallow him up to his armpits. I know that although he will be clean when the bath is done, it will be more by accident than impulse. The swirling water of a great summer storm at sea will wash away the last adventure but give life to the next. When Aaron emerges, his wrinkled fingers and toes will be trying to mop up the tsunami that jumped the sea walls and spilled onto the floor.

I put on a DVD in my room for the kids to watch for a little while. As they curl up on my bed and snuggle into the big pillows, Ms. Frizzle guides the Magic School Bus along some adventure through the digestive system while I go out to make dinner. I am desperate just to get through the day without anything else to clean up or conquer.

I wince as I hear the commotion begin to rise after a while as the educational fun has given way to slapstick and they both roll around laughing at the shenanigans of Tom and Jerry. I speed up a bit, but just as I am about to put the plates on the table, a thunderous crash sounds from the bedroom. I rush in, fearing what I might find.

When I get there, I find Aaron dazed and confused in a heap on the floor with the cross rail of the four-poster bed broken in two. He's not even crying yet because he's too stunned but not really hurt. I pick him up—he's seven but still easy enough to hoist. I am befuddled. The post is nearly four inches in girth! The kid only weighs forty-five pounds, but nonetheless here we all are amidst the splinters. Apparently, Aaron was just tall enough to walk tightrope-style across the rail with his hands touching the ceiling for balance. In hindsight I'm kind of sorry I missed this stunt. He bursts into tears, bawling his apology over and over. I fain disapproval, but mostly I am just glad that we aren't headed for the emergency room again. *Is it bedtime yet?* I wonder.

Aaron has sent us to the emergency room four times over the course of his short life so far. When he was two he climbed onto a rickety little table that gave way under his weight and tipped. He hit his face just under his nose and to this day has a small white line of a scar about a half inch long above his upper lip. When he was five years old we were staying in a vacation condo and he emerged from a bubble bath and went streaking naked through the living room, tripped and split his scalp just behind his left ear. He was granted 5 staples to close that wound. At six he took a chunk out of the corner of his jaw when his roller skates went out from under him and he fell onto an elevated sprinkler head, we probably should have gone to visit the good doctors for that one too. But that one at least seemed debatable. At eight-years-old, he and a pack of cub scouts were playing tag in the cafeteria after their meeting and apparently running around on the slick linoleum in your sock feet is a good way to slip and put a sizable gash in your chin.

He got nine stitches for that one, and another visible scar to prove it. To date, the most significant and impressive visit to the emergency room was the result of a run-in with a brick wall. Aaron lost control of his bike, which sent him sailing into a brick wall in the park behind our house. He broke his left forearm, and tore a sizable split in the side of his knee. This encounter required 12 stitches in his knee, a cast, and provided a scar he will be able to tell stories about for the rest of his life, no doubt. The timing on this particular injury occurred 2 days before we were to leave on our cross country road trip to San Francisco. It's a little hard to hang off a cable car with only one good arm. He spent the summer trying not to sink in swimming pools weighted down by the black fiberglass cast. At least they put waterproof padding in the cast. That helped a lot with our summer plans. I would like to avoid any more visits to our emergency facilities for a while.

I am glad the days' excitement did not land us in the ER again and when the boys are finally asleep, I am left to my thoughts, and I re-evaluate the episodes of the day. I have spent many hours in the screaming pain of silent desperation. I have spent enough time trying to place blame on myself and on Brett, who is off at work.

At the same time I am quite content and embrace the silent house. It's a refuge for me after a long day. This is *my* time. In my empty bed I allow myself to be mindful of the actions and changes I have recently witnessed in Brett. I feel the healing that is well underway but is a constant effort. I am quite guarded but very hopeful. It is a pleasure to discover again, who we are and what we mean to each other.

Nights are always the same. When the day is done for me, Brett is still at work. He won't return until 4:00 AM or 5:00 AM, and I have long since stopped even hearing him come in even though the garage opens just behind our bedroom wall. Now if the kids cough or snivel, I'm awake. Survival instincts, I guess. Justin has gone to bed easily as always. Aaron has negotiated one last kiss, hug, cup of water, and trip to the toilet and is restlessly trying to figure out what else he might need besides sleep. I make the nightly rounds to repack lunches and backpacks. I throw the pillows back onto the couch and put all the wayward action heroes back in the toy boxes that are strategically placed in various hot zones around the house.

Falling in love again with someone so close is a remarkable journey. It is both familiar and unknown. I feel empowered by Brett's bravery and conviction these last few months. I have seen him accomplish things of which I never thought him capable. It's too soon to trust what I feel, but this is a process, and forgiveness is a choice.

Forgiveness is the first step down this new path on which we'll embark together. We are stronger now that we ever were. We know more about ourselves and each other than we would have otherwise. I certainly didn't ask for this trial, nor any of the rest, but it has helped to shape who we are becoming, isn't to be dismissed with regret.

Brett's and my strange and uneasy summer faded breezily into fall. With great effort, active forgiveness, and patient hearts we began to grow together again for the first time in many years. There was a peace about us that had been previously unreachable. It was intangible but certain. Brett and I were beginning to become the people we had forgotten to be.

Although we had had time and distance to allow healing to begin, there was a lifetime of work yet to do. I was trying to be a little selfish, a difficult feat for me, by learning to insist on some time and space of my own. I encouraged Brett to handle the boys sometimes without my help, and he routinely took the boys off one at a time to do things that they enjoy. For example, Justin loves interesting trivia facts so Brett took him to the Ripley's Believe it Or Not, and Aaron loves hockey so Brett took him on the train to the L.A. Kings game. He took me on dates, too, somewhere quiet where we could talk, eat, and laugh. On date nights, we both have experiences and honesty to bring to the table, and we have genuine interest in and a greater respect for each other. We have learned too well that complacency leads down dangerous paths.

Some days, I'm sure we won't always have the imagination, intuition, or patience to wade through the most obvious problems and find the gifts of a situation. Hopefully, we will take turns at least most of the time because it's all about sharing perspective. Brett helps me remember that Aaron, the same little green-eyed boy who during a tantrum just slammed his door so hard that the photos fell off their nails, is the same little boy who silently wrote everyone a Christmas note and hid it in each of our stockings just to tell us he loves us. He is the same little boy who wants to curl up close to snuggle every night while we read. He is the same little boy who wraps up his own little toys to give to his big brother as gifts. I help Brett to see when he goes in to read with Justin at bedtime and Justin brings out the hockey yearbook, that it was a gesture meant entirely for Brett because Justin has no interest in hockey, but he knows his dad does. Considering someone else's feelings and desires doesn't come naturally for Justin. It takes a lot of work for him to tune in that well, and that deserves recognition. I hope to help Brett see these little things that might otherwise be taken for granted.

What rich experience this all adds to life. You really can't appreciate the very good days without having lived in the very bad days. How much sweeter is the reward that comes from an arduous path. How can I expect to fathom the greatest joys in life without having first worked so hard for them?

At the end of the day if I am unable to forgive things that seemingly don't deserve to be, then there is no freedom for me. To be trapped by the feelings of anger and self-pity is stifling. There is no room for progress without forgiveness. To forgive is not to forget, but to use what you have learned to become more complete. Forgiveness takes time, and it doesn't fall upon you like a wave of relief. Given enough time, you can choose to do it.

I recognize that when Justin talks back, I acknowledge the fact that at least he is able to do so. I recognize that even though I have left things undone, it was because more pressing things were at stake. I recognize that although Aaron can blaze with fury, he also loves with the same fire. I recognize that while Brett's path may have veered off for a while, in the end he voluntarily chose the one that lead back to his family.

There will always be imperfections, disillusionment, and disappointments; however, there is great beauty and strength to be found in letting the disenchanted feelings go and replacing them with the expectation that there is, in fact, a reason and a purpose for the uneven terrain.

Chapter Seven

Stomping in Puddles

Wading through the Options to find what Works

I made a mad dash for the car. It took about three strides to cover the fifteen feet between the shelter and the car, and I was already well on my way to wringing wet. The rain was shooting down in drops the size of grapes and bouncing six inches off the ground before flooding the pavement. I folded quickly into the car and wrestled to get the door closed only to realize that Aaron, then, eight-years-old, was still out in the rain. He was oblivious to the obvious dilemma I faced. I took a deep breath to call to him through the storm, but my eyes fell on his expression. His head was tilted back in laughter, and his arms were outstretched, welcoming the engulfing deluge that was saturating him so quickly. His little feet and bright eyes danced as he looked at me gasping through the shower, rain running fast off his nose and eyelashes. My monologue imploring him to get into the car was momentarily silenced by the wish that there were more times in life when we could all experience such simple bliss.

As Aaron got into the car, his head was still swimming with his escapade. I tried my best to sound irritated as he slipped across the leather seats and left muddy footprints on the floor mats, but mostly I was thankful for the reminder that not everything has to fit into a conventional box. Sometimes even though we learn that we are supposed to walk around the rain puddles, it is often better to trudge right through—or at least lighten up even when the rain doesn't.

The rain was thundering down on the roof of the car, and the windows steamed up from our damp bodies. Aaron was giggling and reeling, his clothes clinging to his frame. The wipers were having trouble keeping up with the rain as we headed home. I wished I could approach more of life's downpours with as much vigor and exuberance as Aaron does. Aaron is a constant reminder of how to jump in with both feet. His love of life is infectious and inviting.

The thought then crossed my mind that Justin wouldn't have enjoyed this romp at all. He would have felt quite violated by the rain, and he would have been decidedly irritated. I frowned as I thought of his horrified reaction to our description of being "soaked to the bone," an idiom he wouldn't be able to interpret because he is so literal. (For him it's horrible to imagine that he might laugh his head off, that the cat might have his tongue, that I will keep an eye on him, that I will give him a hand, or that his heart could break. Ever stop to think about the things we say off the cuff and then try to actually explain them? It's quite a challenge.)

I remember one night when Justin was about eight years old, I closed his blinds, and gazed for a moment at the tiniest sliver of a waning crescent moon.

"Tomorrow is a new moon," I told him. I turned around to kiss him good night and found his little face clouding over and tears forming at the rim of his eyelids. I gathered him up in my lap. "What's wrong?"

He looked at me tearfully and said, "I'm really gonna miss the old moon."

So many things to explain.

One of the most difficult things I have tried to explain to Justin is sarcasm. How do you explain that one to an eight-year-old whose world is black and white? It is appropriately defined as cutting language or remarks that mean the opposite of what they seem to say and are intended to mock or deride. For example, when someone says, "Oh, great!" they usually mean the opposite—but not always. Justin came home from school one day and told me he had heard that word and he asked me what it meant. I explained it as best I could and then spent weeks and months using little bits of sarcasm in an exaggerated way, and most days he would catch my drift and exclaim "hey! You are doing that thing with that weird word again, right!?"

There are so many things we take for granted that don't seem to make any sense when you stop to think about them, or worse yet, try to explain them to someone whose mind doesn't work that way. There are even words that don't really have the same meaning anymore. You certainly wouldn't want to announce that you felt "gay" if you only mean you're happy, nor would you suggest something was "queer" just because it was puzzling. But how do you explain this to a pre-adolescent who only understands language in its definitive form? Justin is just about as far from politically correct as you can expect to find. It's a part of his charm really, and so the challenge rages on.

Justin also is a very visual learner. He hears you just fine but often doesn't completely process what he's being told unless you can show him as well. He thinks in pictures and memorizes things as if his mind has taken a photo. When he was five and Aaron was two, we found ourselves in Maui driving along the coast admiring the clean water foaming up as the waves dashed the rocks below. We were listening to the narration of a story tape being recited from the tapedeck. The road wound around, clinging to the cliffs. The rocks that threatened to fall atop passing rental cars were discouraged by chain link that lined the roadside although every so often we could find a few that had outwitted the fences' embrace and tumbled onto the path, requiring constant vigilance in our journey. The story was interrupted only by the chime that indicated that the kids needed to turn the page of the book as they followed along with the story teller. When the story ended, it was replaced by Justin's own rendition. Justin chatted away happily to himself in the backseat while Brett and I admired the beautiful day punctuated by the black rocks, fine sand beaches, and turquoise water. It didn't occur to me at first to focus on his little monologue but after a few minutes it became clear to me that I was missing another clear picture of just how visual Justin's mind is. As I listened more closely, I began to 'see' the words just like Justin was. I could tell he was reading off a page in his mind.

At five years old, Justin's language was still very hard to interpret unless he was able to show you what he meant. So when he started throwing letters about, I asked him to repeat it, unsure of whether he was trying to spell something. At first he seemed to think he had done something wrong, and I had to reassure him it was a good thing before he would repeat himself. So he reiterated, "N-I-T-S-U-J." In print it seems a lot clearer, but that morning it took me a while to unravel the little puzzle in my head. Then I was astounded. Justin didn't offer me insight into his mind very often, and this was a great opportunity. I started giving him more words that I knew he could spell, and he spelled them all to me backward. Brett and I exchanged incredulous smiles. I tried to challenge him with tougher words, but everything I threw at him he threw back in mirror image as if he were reading the letters backward right off a page. I knew he could see the word in his head, and it explained a lot about how best to reach him. Want him to learn something new? Give him an image to study or a figure to hold. It will become part of his database—forward and back.

Justin remembers not only what he learned, but quite often where he learned it and what year it was. The fun comes in trying to inspire Justin to offer enough pieces of the picture in clear enough detail that I can begin to see things through his eyes. I remember once after September 11 that Justin was reflective and sad at the loss. He was remembering aloud having been in New York when he was six. It took me a while to follow because I didn't want to contradict him—yet we had never been to New York. I learned very early on that if Justin told me something, it was the truth in one way or another. Instead of telling him he was mistaken, I tried to get into his head. He mentioned buying a big cinnamon pretzel and walking around while he ate it. That did it. It dawned on me like a great revelation: he *did* remember being in New York—well, at New York New York in Las Vegas! For him it was the same place.

Aaron is less disjointed but more of a challenge in many ways. He is more straightforward, more likely to intentionally lead you astray if he is so moved, and more animated about the stories he tells. In fact, he is more animated about everything he does than just about anyone else I have met. But even for him there are emotions and compartments that he hasn't figured out how to unlock, and he stays trapped in the turmoil of it. When he was in kindergarten, his newly married teacher shared with her class that she was going to have a baby and that she was due just before the end of the year. The kids were very happy for her, but I am not sure any of them understood that she would be leaving before the end of term. As it turned out, she delivered early and didn't return from spring break as she had intended. She never really got to prepare the kids for her leaving; she didn't get to introduce the new teacher or give her a seal of approval. She didn't get to say good-bye.

The new teacher was fresh out of school, and, funny enough, she was our dentist's daughter. She was dropped into a class of unprepared five- and six-year-olds who all felt like they had been robbed of their best friend without warning or explanation. I think Aaron challenged her the most. He seemed to hold her personally responsible for the atrocity. I spoke to the kind woman with the quizzical look of disorientation on her face. I wondered if the expression was permanent. I reassured her she was doing well, and I would reinforce with Aaron that she was the new teacher and that he needed to settle down in class and let her teach.

On one particularly rocky afternoon, Aaron and I sat on the couch and tried to unfold the misery of the day. He sat accusing this interloper of causing all the problems he was having. I listened carefully.

When he was done, I remember saying, "Aaron, I can see that you are very angry with your teacher."

He disagreed and said he liked Mrs. Little.

I responded, "No, Aaron. You are very angry with Mrs. Faye for leaving you."

At that, he burst into tears and sobbed like I had never seen before. He had felt abandoned by a special force in his life. I held him and told him it was okay to feel how he felt. I told him that being angry was okay but being mean wasn't. I helped him to see how Mrs. Little was new to this, too, and just as scared as he was, that she really needed his help to feel comfortable, and that she was doing a good job. He learned that Mrs. Faye still loved him, but she had been surprised when the baby had come early, and she had to stay home now to take care of him. (Mrs. Faye eventually came and visited the class, but by that time Aaron had made his peace.)

In that afternoon, Aaron's path changed and his kindergarten career was no longer about derailing Mrs. Little in an attempt to regain Mrs. Faye. They never had a single other conflict. Aaron was a model student for her and was always happy to see her and eager to please. They had found their common ground, and Aaron really liked her after all. It was never really about her anyway, of course. She too became one of his favorite teachers of all time. In one of my many desperate ventures into behavioral therapy, a wise person once told me, "Acknowledge the feeling, and the behavior will change." Go figure, it works.

We have spent a lot of time trying to find ways directly through the middle of issues that arise because skirting them only seems to add to the cumulative problems. Every obstacle appears to me to be another opportunity to gain the knowledge and experience of resolution. What good does it do to avoid things from which you can learn? These things are put in place as sample tests so that when something seemingly insurmountable comes along, you're already equipped with the tools acquired on earlier quests. Expect to get wet when you stomp into the middle of a puddle left from a downpour in life but also expect to grow.

There are so many opportunities in life to appreciate what the storms bring with them. Take the time to enjoy the immeasurable joy that a dance in summer shower can bring and forget about the water pooling in the foot-well of the backseat. Does it really matter if the carpet gets damp or if there is one more load of laundry to do? The intoxicating spirit of wild abandon becomes evermore elusive. Delight in the fleeting moments you are witnessing. Better yet, jump right in. I have found that a change in perspective is all it takes to turn a situation from frustrating to enlightening. I try to take all the opportunities I can find to appreciate my children rather than criticize them. Admittedly, some days it is harder than others.

Justin is quite independent. He enjoys accomplishing things on his own. He rarely asks for help, undoubtedly a combination of a lack of social inclination and a self-determined spirit. Nonetheless, he grows with every accomplishment. Sometimes it's a marvel to watch him as he goes through whatever steps are required. He often looks as though he is completing his task quite by accident. I seem to follow him around ready to catch things as they are unknowingly knocked askew, mop up spills, and catch falling knick-knacks. The funny thing is that as uncalculated as his movements appear to be, he actually has pretty good luck at getting the things done that he needs to do. Watch him pour milk into his glass, and you would swear it's going to breach the rim. The milk flows in with such force that I have often found myself grabbing for a dish towel only to find that somehow not a drop had gone astray. His hands often flail in some unknown orchestration, yet the leaded glass panels on the buffet remain unscathed.

It has taken some time for me to learn to back off, not worry what might happen at every turn, and simply let some of the mishaps occur. I have had plenty of experience with the "what might happen" department, and it ain't all pretty. Still, an ounce of prevention might be worth a pound of cure, but an ounce of experience is worth its weight in gold. After all, I'm not really raising boys; I am raising men. And as I'm often reminded, "Everyone makes mistakes, Mom."

And sometimes Justin makes them. Justin is fond of reminding me that his name means "justice," and he isn't against wielding his own form, which occasionally resembles vigilantism. Justin feels he must seek vindication if he has been wronged, and we're working on that. One such occasion arose during a T-ball game many years ago. During the first of three innings, the catcher tagged out Justin as he headed for home. There are no outs in T-ball, and Justin knew it. I felt bad for the catcher, who was only doing what his overbearing coach had asked him to do. (The coach had wanted his team to practice all the major league rules even if they had no place on the T-ball field.)

That same coach had also provided full catcher gear so the kid was well protected, but still I didn't feel that I could let Justin bulldoze him. I knew Justin was mad, and I was worried because he is notorious for holding a grudge.

As the second inning progressed, I got up and met Justin out near home plate to guide him, cheer him on, and guard the catcher. The poor kid was a sitting duck as Justin barreled into home. It was a near miss, but no harm was done.

The third inning brought in a new catcher. There was a brief timeout while the new kid geared up for the last inning. I relaxed a bit and settled in to visit with the other parents and cheer the kids on. Justin was on base, and I had just started getting the snacks ready for the little ballplayers for after the game. I then realized with a sudden twinge of horror that Justin had probably completely missed the fact that the catcher was a new kid. He was adorned in the same gear and looked the same as the villain who had started this course toward retribution. I dropped what I was doing and ran but knew as I rounded the chain-link fence that I was too far away. I watched helplessly as the freight train that was Justin, sped down the track and collided full force with the pint-sized, unsuspecting athlete. They both sprawled across home plate in dusty red heap. I looked back at Brett and my friends who seemed confused as to how I knew to run even if it had been a little late. They didn't seem to understand why Justin held such ill will for the new catcher. They didn't realize Justin had no idea it was a *new* catcher.

The other team accepted that it was just a vigorous kid trying to make it home and took it as one of those collisions that occurs at the plate from time to time. Thankfully, the game ended without any more major incidents. I took Justin aside and caught him up on the change in lineup. He was fine after that. I also tried to help him see that his out didn't count anyway and that the kid was only doing what his coach told him to do. But that was pointless. For Justin, who deals in logic, it was illogical to make up new rules that went against the set rules for T-ball so it was a moot point.

In an effort to increase the opportunities for success, we have used numerous charts and visual aids as part of our arsenal. I want the boys to feel ownership in their accomplishments. I want them to see where they are growing. I want them to be able to think one step ahead without my having to tell them. I want them to be proud of what they did. When Justin was about three or so, I made his first chart because we were having a lot of trouble with the bedtime routine. Justin just couldn't seem to get through the evening without melting, so I helped him understand the process through visual aids. He had his own chart with pictures of himself taking a bath, brushing his teeth, using the potty, putting his pajamas on, and reading bedtime stories. He loved to look at himself in the pictures and always wanted to do what he saw himself doing. I laminated some of his favorite stickers and applied Velcro to their backs and to the chart. Every night as he achieved a task, he got to pick a sticker and stick it on. It really helped him process the routine as well as give him ownership of the achievements. He stopped giving me a hard time, and by the time he was settled into bed, he knew he had done everything he needed to do. Things ran a lot smoother after that.

We made similar charts for Aaron because he always has trouble calming down and tends to lash out quickly. He and I talked about things that he could do to help himself calm down. He came up with his own ideas, like going for a walk, jumping up and down, hitting a pillow, and taking deep breaths. We took pictures and put them up on display. He could look at them and think about better ways to let off steam. The problem was, of course, by the time he was that mad, the last thing he really wanted to do was calm down. Apparently, there is a biological rush that goes along with real anger, and somehow a cardboard happy chart just fails to completely help in these instances. It was more of a reminder of the day-to-day disorder and mild disturbances. His charts help some, but five years later, we are still working on ways to help Aaron calm down.

Some difficulties can't be overcome with charts, and we look to currency to get the result we need. Aaron might be the fastest kid on the block, but he is painfully slow at getting himself situated in the car and buckled in. He always needs to "just gotta" do something. Every car trip was delayed by crawling minutes while he settled in. It wasn't as simple as snapping him in myself because he needed to make himself do it. He wanted the right; he just couldn't get to it, so I made a bet with him one day. I told him I bet I could get in and get my seatbelt fastened before he did. I told him that every time he beat me, I would give him a quarter—"seatbelt quarters" is what we called them. He racked up quite a few over the course of a couple of months. Before long he forgot about the quarters, and it simply became a habit to get his seatbelt on quickly. Score one point for Mom!

We also established a chore chart and listed about twenty-five things that the boys could do to earn money. Some chores were easy. Some required them to learn a new skill, like working the washer or dryer. Some required some actual manual labor, like shoveling snow or raking leaves. Most were the ones they were used to, like making their beds and taking out the trash. For each one they can earn a dollar or so to put toward something they would like to have. The reasons this worked well were multifold: I didn't feel the need to buy little things for which they asked, I equipped them with the ability to earn enough money to buy things for themselves, and they learned to value the money they earned as well as the things they purchased because they had worked for it. At the beginning they certainly worked hard toward earning a lot more money than they previously had, but they also learned some new things along the way.

We have recently run into trouble with Aaron, who tends to be a terrible procrastinator, not following through on things he is asked to do until one of us is quite upset with him. He will put something off until he has to do it at a breakneck pace to be completed in time. It's almost like that rush—or his mother yelling at him—motivates him. Of course, that isn't the way anyone really wants to go through life. I remember the words a medical doctor and an expert on ADHD emphasized in a session I attended, "Don't be your child's Ritalin." I had never thought of it that way, but yelling and spanking both eventually deliver the same compliance that medication does. The rush from the adrenaline release in a child under the pressure of being yelled at or spanked is chemically the equivalent to what the medication would have done but without the fuss and feud. We had to look for a way to get Aaron cued in on doing something quickly, and his currency seems to be—well—currency, or first time dollars. First time dollars are doled out for tasks that are completed the first time either of the kids is asked to do it. We offer greater rewards for things completed *before* they have been asked. Again, this is a method of positive reinforcement that will phase out as habit replaces the desire for the cash. The novelty always wears off, but hopefully, the new self-motivation will remain at least for a while. I have used such ploys to help get them through anything from getting ready for bed to picking up after themselves. The cajoling ceases, the compliance increases, and more gets done at least for a while.

There is no doubt that we will all get hit with downpours in life. We will, from time to time, feel like we might drown. We will feel like we don't want to wade through any more puddles, that we are too grown up, and that there must be a better way than getting soaked.

Sometimes there just isn't a better path and life requires us to get wet. There isn't a better way to handle something except to stand in the rain and dance like my son showed me that day. Flexibility and creativity are key. I have to remind myself not to get stuck in what I think *should* work best with these boys, but to continually be willing to revise my approach until I find what *does* work best. Most often, what they need most isn't written in a bestselling book, and it isn't part of the doctor's regimen or the schools recommendations. I have to always play to whatever strengths are most apparent at the time.

There is something rich and welcoming about the spirit in which a child spins with his arms outstretched in roaring rainstorm while lakes form around his ankles. Shouldn't all of us spend some time doing just that? I don't remember the last time I ran into the rain just to feel it splash across my face. Maybe I was too hasty to get into the car. Maybe I missed an opportunity to enjoy life just a little more. I think our children might have just as much to teach us as we think we have to teach them. But if it starts to hail, sometimes you do have to duck and cover until the worst of it passes.

There are undoubtedly things that will continue to create unwelcome situations. Murphy's Law has fast become part of our everyday philosophies and expectations. If we already know that, then I expect it's about time we start putting a new face to the fury. When did we stop looking for the humor in life's unforeseen maladies?

I remember dropping an entire bowl of generously buttered, hot baby peas a few weeks ago. As it slipped from my fingers, I jumped back so the Pyrex bowl wouldn't connect with my toe. As I unclenched my jaw and opened my eyes, I saw the starry field of slippery peas rolling their way into the nether regions of the kitchen; trapped forever by the waiting refrigerator, stove, and dishwasher; and forever imprisoned by their steel sentries. All eyes watched to see what I might do or say. I took the challenge and threw the dish towel on top of them exclaiming, "I didn't want peas anyway, did you guys? No veggies tonight!" I let a broad grin find its way to my lips and sat down to dinner with the boys, who were relieved that there was no real upset, pleased there were no peas, and witnessed a better way to handle one of life's little chaotic moments. We let the peas sit there while we finished dinner, and then we all got to work to find as many of the little elusive buggers as we could. So I spent more time than I wanted to trying to clean my floor, but you should have seen the sheen! Lesson learned? Find more humor in the ample supply of mishaps and encounters that trip us up every day.

Chapter Eight

The joy of Treading Barefoot over Legos

Running across the Improbable Building Blocks of Humor

My dad had always impressed upon me what social etiquette was expected. There simply are things that are acceptable and things that are not, and ne'er the two shall meet. Grandpa, my dad's dad, was an aviator and a navy captain. There were certain unbendable expectations of such a family. Grandpa was a kind man—as is my dad—but still there were fairly set expectations. Officers or their wives would come to call, and there was a definite order to how the visit would flow right down to the appropriate length of time that the social engagement should last. Kids, of course, were also expected to display appropriate manners and niceties as well. It was the long lost days of being "seen and not heard."

Dad adopted a certain amount of naval conduct in his own style. I'm sure it was completely unavoidable, and I'm not so sure that it was so misplaced. I learned an awful lot about class and how to show you have a little from both of them. I don't think he actually ever ran a white-gloved finger along my bookcase, but I think he was tempted. I do believe he did attempt to bounce a quarter off my bed though. As I recall, it wasn't very successful. I'm sticking to my belief that that only works on army bunks, not Sealy, Simmons, or Serta.

I remember when Justin was about four years old, Brett, the boys, and I were at a pancake house for breakfast. Aaron was in his high chair, and Justin, who had been waiting patiently for his food, discovered the booth seat was bouncy and began jumping up and down on the seat. I was alarmed and ecstatic at the same time. My head echoed a distant reprimand, "Children shouldn't stand, let alone jump, on the seats in a restaurant"—(thanks, Dad)—but my heart was hollering "Break through!" He had never jumped before, not anywhere, not ever! This was something most kids were able to do by three years old, but Justin had never before been able to organize his mind and body well enough to coordinate any sort of a jump. Both feet had never left the planet's surface at the same time before! The bouncy seat didn't hurt, but still it was a huge first. I reveled at this accomplishment, which had eluded him for so long, and I sat in awe until the proper etiquette recitation in my head was impossible to ignore any further. Then I congratulated him and asked him to sit for his breakfast, which he did without any further antics. It was such a funny place to feel caught. I am quite sure that the patrons and staff of the $2.99 pancake house have seen a lot worse than a preschooler using his bench for a trampoline. But I wondered if anyone among them had ever witnessed a miracle before and if any of them even knew they had that day. I'm sure they were completely unaware. But *I* knew.

I suppose it's reassuring to realize that we do actually retain a lot of what we are taught in our early lives. It's nice to become aware that what I try to instill in the boys doesn't entirely fall on deaf ears and that as we grow and mature, we are still the children we once were in some ways and we have brought all life's lessons with us. Still, it might be a blessing that we allow some of it to slip away. I hope the kids don't retain every detail. What a scary thought that is.

Presumably the endless hours we spend in occupational therapy were beginning to pay off. All that time the therapists spent rolling Justin in the pillow, sailing him down the ramp on a scooter board, bouncing him on a mini-trampoline, and having him walk across the balance beam seemed to be starting to matter. These techniques that were helping him to understand his body better were starting to make a difference. The therapists found wonderful and fun ways to help Justin with his sensory integration problems. While the other kids at preschool could ride a trike and bounce a ball, Justin couldn't. While they could thread spools and macaroni onto yarn to make necklaces, Justin couldn't. Slowly though, all the work, time, and energy were beginning to show up in his daily life.

It's very frustrating and saddening to watch your friends' children move so far ahead and so out of Justin's reach. You want so desperately to enjoy their children's accomplishments, but you can't really join into the enthusiasm. You want to taste it, too. You watch the little girls and boys look at every detail of something and carefully color inside the lines. You watch them engage their peers, their teachers, and their parents. You watch them snuggle and look for comfort. You watch them want to share something, a toy or an experience they love. You watch them care for their dolls or become their favorite superhero. You even envy the way they want their parents to put a bandage on the tiniest of scratches.

Justin wouldn't request a bandage if he had hit an artery. He couldn't care less about taking care of something or needing comfort. I remember once after school, he came home and sat on the couch so I could help him take off his shoes: this shoe, that shoe, that sock, this sock. But on that last foot, I noticed an angry swollen area next to the nail of his big toe. It was infected, and there was a swelling full of green pus. He had an ingrown toenail and hadn't been the least bit bothered by it. Presumably the worst had come up quickly because it hadn't been noticeable before now to the eye, but I would have thought at least that *he* would have noticed. But he didn't because he doesn't feel pain like everyone else. He objected to it only when his eyes fell on it. He then knew it looked like a sore and seemed to mind.

I settled him down with a favorite video and went to collect the antiseptic, a sterile needle, the toenail clippers, and a band-aid. I cut the nail and removed the imbedded piece. I opened and drained the abscess; I disinfected the lesion with Betadine and applied the bandage. He never even looked over to see what I was doing. He didn't need my comfort even then. I'm not sure you ever stop feeling a little robbed of that.

There are a few things I find hard to let go of. Christmas is the biggest. I go through the motions of having Justin hang his stocking and help put out cookies and milk on Christmas Eve. I read *The Night before Christmas* while Brett stomps on the roof and jingles the sleigh bells. I kiss Justin good night and falsely anticipate he will have trouble falling asleep. In the morning I go in and wake him up to tell him it's Christmas morning. He stumbles out and seats himself at the table for breakfast. What kid oversleeps on Christmas and then wants breakfast before presents? Mine does.

Aaron's presence has helped restore that balance, and as time has gone by, Justin has gotten right on board with all of the magic and mayhem of Christmas. Aaron can't wait to follow all the traditions, has trouble falling asleep, and can't wait to get up and at 'em. Justin has learned to follow suit.

My rewards were different, but they were just as powerful. I've often sought solace in the belief that when we work so hard toward a goal even if it's just jumping a few inches in the air, the accomplishment, when achieved, is that much more profound. It means more than if it had come too easy.

Have you ever seen a Jack Russell terrier—the little white and brown spotted dog—tugging relentlessly on a sock? (Forgive the metaphor; I was a vet technician in a former life.) Just when it seems they may lose their grip, they manage to readjust and clamp down their impervious jaws tighter still. They hold on with such a determined, one-minded force that everything else in the world seemingly ceases to exist.

Welcome to the world of autism.

There often seems to be one thing whose status exists above all else—one thing that commands every thought. Every waking moment would be spent thinking, talking about, manipulating, considering, embracing, reiterating, and reciting. It's different for every individual, but the steadfast hold is the same. The object of obsession might even change begrudgingly over time, but the need for fixation remains a constant.

We have maneuvered through Sodor Island where we all became intimately acquainted with Thomas and his friends. The little blue tank engine was as much a part of Justin's family than any of the rest of us for a time. Endless hours were spent trudging over the clickety-clack tracks, up over hill and dale, and through windy tunnels, and stopping only briefly to take on water or unload troublesome trucks. I always knew where Justin was. He was on the island figuratively and actually. I can't say he acted out great adventures of his own design, but he could re-enact the recorded episodes flawlessly.

In fact, it was around this time—around his third birthday—that I started getting the idea that he could read. The videotapes were identical with the exception of the words on them. There were no images or pictures, only words, but Justin always knew exactly which one he wanted to see. He would look at them until he decided on one. If I asked him to get me one by name, he found it every time. He at least knew how the words looked on the tape cartridge of the stories he had memorized. That's how he learned to read. He memorized the way words looked, but he wouldn't be able to read phonetically for many more years. He didn't have to and still prefers not to.

When Justin learned to speak long after his third birthday, we would converse in the language of trains. That is to say, he would offer single words, and I would need to fill in the rest through experience and trial and error. Justin wouldn't put two words together for many more months. At this time, his best friends, the miniature trains— Percy, Duck, and James—were my best friends, too. They had found a way to encourage Justin to speak when I couldn't. I wouldn't hesitate to argue that a fascination turned obsession could be unhealthy, but I also wouldn't dismiss the fact that anything that is a strong currency can be used in your favor.

So, the little magnetic trains went everywhere: the bath, to bed, and the sandbox. (Did you know there is a whole lot of iron in sand? Just try to clean it off a magnetic train coupler.) Slowly through the use of the trains, we began to draw more and more language out of the little guy. One day while working with Michael, the speech therapist, Justin was playing trains, and he wanted to add more engines to the track. Michael had the box of trains and wanted Justin to ask for them. Justin could say, "Ag-in," which he used for anything he wanted to do again or have more of. So in an attempt to get Justin to say the word *more,* Richard repeated, "Mo," over and over until Justin began to answer in kind. He could say, "Mo." However, when Michael said, "More," we found that Justin couldn't produce the *r* sound in this combination yet. Instead, it came out as a long-awaited and much-anticipated word that took my breath away. Justin said, "Mom," for the first time ever.

In that moment I froze and held Justin in my gaze. My breath caught in my chest, my eyes welled, and a hard impassable lump closed my throat. Once again, the world stood still just for me. I listened to Michael continue to say, "More," delicately imploring Justin to do the same. He obviously had missed the miracle. My voice cracked and returned. Quietly I hushed Michael and rested my hand on his arm. He looked over at me. I smiled at him and asked him to move on to a new word—*Mom.* I had waited an eternity to hear my son call my name. Even if he didn't mean it for me just yet, it would do for now.

Over the years we have used the latest craze to work in our favor. Although there is plenty of time for free play, there is also a very useful side to something held so dear. Justin has long since outgrown

Thomas and the little island although every so often he will pick up an old book. He has moved on to trivia facts about anything scientific or animal related. He has learned the ways of the Jedi, and he has incorporated Pokemon and Yu-Gi-Oh—much to my chagrin—into his repertoire for the last several years. I can't even begin to illustrate how much I miss that cheeky little tank engine when compared to Pika-whoever.

But it doesn't matter what he holds tight to as long as I can also use it to benefit him. It works well as the proverbial carrot, and we all need a reason to work hard for something. A few more minutes on the Game Cube or a new trading card works pretty well to encourage growth around here. It's a versatile currency that can be doled out in varying degrees to encourage anything from acceptable behavior to better language skills. Remember the look in the dog's eyes from which you just managed to get the sock away? Well, he would do anything for you to give it back. Whether man or beast, we all hold something dear and will work hard to have it for just a little while longer. You use what works.

However, having said that I'm hesitant to incorporate Justin's most recent interest, which is "bikini girls." I have caught him leafing through my clothes magazines in hopes of falling upon a swimsuit or an underwear advertisement. I'm told this is a perfectly normal infatuation for a budding preteen boy of twelve years old. Oh sure, for *this* he chooses to be normal. It figures!

He has even gone so far as to write out a very interesting computer game that you could play, which highlights girls wearing bikinis of different colors, indicating what powers or strengths they might have. The enchantment of something so seductive seems to have spurred on this newfound interest in expressing himself in script, and at least his creative writing skills are improving.

The concern is that he might become obsessed or at the very least be unable to conceal the obsession like typical boys his age learn to do over time. Although I know his interest is quite age appropriate and probably one of the strongest currencies I will ever be able to wield, I don't imagine I will ever use the Victoria's Secret catalog or the *Sports Illustrated* Swimsuit Issue as a motivator. I suppose there must be limits to this methodology.

When the kids are at school or sleeping, the house is quiet, and the walls have ceased to vibrate for the moment, I trail around collecting odds and ends that have been left in middle of battle, escapade, or entanglement. The children are absent in body, but their little spirits dance around the house as lively as ever. Their voices echo through the halls, and the toys wait eagerly to be put into action again. It's impossible to stride across the floors without colliding with at least one armament.

As I refill the boxes with their missing contents of cars, Legos, magic castle knights and dragons, Star Wars heroes and villains, and Pokemon figurines, I realize I am smiling. I have managed to reclaim the house that my husband and I pretend belongs to us. The sole of my foot still stings from a recent encounter with a well-camouflaged triceratops whose horn found its way through my hide, yet it strikes me as funny. Even when they aren't here, their confidants and sentries defend their turf while they are away. Not only does their spirit linger, but their defense maneuvers, which seem splayed and unintentional, are actually well honed and precise.

I survey the grounds around my feet and decide to leave a few rebels fighting for their cause. I have cleared a safe passage, and that is enough for now. I enjoy looking at the fallen heroes and wonder if they have been defeated or were they instructed to lay low until their commanders' return. I look at the partial Lego works and wonder if the structure was in development or under attack.

There is joy here. There is humor and goodwill. There is love and imagination at play. Why not take the extra minute that you need to see the love, commitment, and fun that went into the chaos around you? After all, it wasn't done with the intent of adding discord to the house or by a naughty child looking for revenge. It was done in the pursuit of great adventure, one that we mostly refuse to take time for anymore.

Some days it's even a struggle to find the time or energy to see. Some days I see only clutter, disarray, or another chore, but today, I am blessed. Today, I see the beauty and the humor in the bedlam.

The house reminds me of the Buddhist temple bells that my grandfather brought back when he was stationed in the South Pacific and have sat on the bookcase at my grandparents' house for decades. Each generation of children learns how to play these small brass cups of varying size; the largest is about the size of your hand. Each sits atop its own little pillow and is accompanied by a small wooden dowel, which is to be rubbed continuously around the outside of bell until the chimes resonate, much like making a wine glass sing by rubbing its rim. They each resound in their own pitch that completely fills the ear, and the vibration carries for a long while even after the dowel has stopped its progression around the bell. The house echoes just as those bells do: The boys might have stopped creating the vibration, but somehow the house still hums its response.

It's so easy to allow the hustle of everyday life and pressure and rush to finish what we must get done drown out that hum. There is great reason to get to that next appointment, pack meeting, or karate belt test; pay the bills, do the laundry, provide suitable food, care for the yard, and keep the house free of mold, mildew, and misplaced merry men. But sometimes there is even a greater need to cancel, slow down, overlook, and regroup. Sometimes we need to exhale and see what we have before us and not get lost in what we have yet to achieve.

I can safely reflect for a few more minutes as I begin to get ready to "enjoy" the rest of the day, the part when the kids come home from school. Somehow, they are much easier to revel in when they are away. It takes great will and concentration to see all the allure when it is being foisted, flailed, and flagrantly put before you. I tidy up my hair to make the trek to Aaron's school. I step gingerly into my tennis shoes because there is still a decided welt where I was impaled by the trihorned Cretaceous creature in the living room. I find that with my foot halfway into my shoe, it can go no farther. I reach in blindly to be met with the south end of a great Matoran. The thorny-looking masked warrior has been taking up residence here for who knows how long. It's difficult to say whether he was hiding from those who pursue him or lying in wait for an unsuspecting victim, but his cover has been blown for now. In the car I strap the wayward Bionicle into Aaron's booster seat, and together we embark on the path that will bring the first of the marauders home.

Aaron, at seven years old, finds it peculiar but enchanting that the Bionicle has made this journey as well. He unclips the seatbelt and settles in next to the squatter. He begins to chatter about his day spent in the company of his best friends and their imaginary companions, boasting names I can't spell or repeat because of their complexity. He beams with his recollection of the day's events and goals achieved. None of what I hear has anything to do with what took place inside his second grade classroom—no mention of *Charlotte's Web* or his subtraction test, but some of the most important learning goes on outside those walls anyway. Although I would also love to hear about his academic achievements, I realize that if those skills need sharpening, we can get out the flashcards, throw spelling words around, read a little more, or, if all else fails, get a tutor. It is much more impossible to teach someone how to be a friend, grow a relationship, or be an integral part of a group. Those lifelong and priceless skills will win half the battle in the long run.

Aaron is always glad when school is out at the end of the day. All the way home I silently navigate the road, but my eyes flit enthusiastically to the rearview mirror, catching fleeting glimpses of those dancing sea green eyes that are heavily framed by long black lashes and capped by the fringe of sandy brown bangs. He shoots glances at the mirror, hoping to punctuate a high point or share with me a moment of enchantment from his day's adventures.

This is one of my favorite parts of every day. He is captive for the moment, and there are no distractions for him. I'm his only audience, and he plays just to me. My injured foot hurts a little less now as I hear more in those ten minutes about the things in his life than I will hear the rest of the day.

I ease off the accelerator just a little. We'll be home soon enough. Let this be mine just a little while longer because tomorrow will bring a great battle and I will need to take all these moments and precious visions as armor into combat.

Tomorrow is our annual IEP. Tomorrow I will take both my children's spirits with me to keep me high and focused as we discuss the upcoming year's goals and objectives based on Justin's deficiencies. That's always a ""great"" time. See. There's that sarcasm again.

Justin graduates to Boy Scouts! 2006

A colorful campout in the living room! 2004

Justin's commencement from 5ᵗʰ grade 2006

Aaron's summer camp 2007

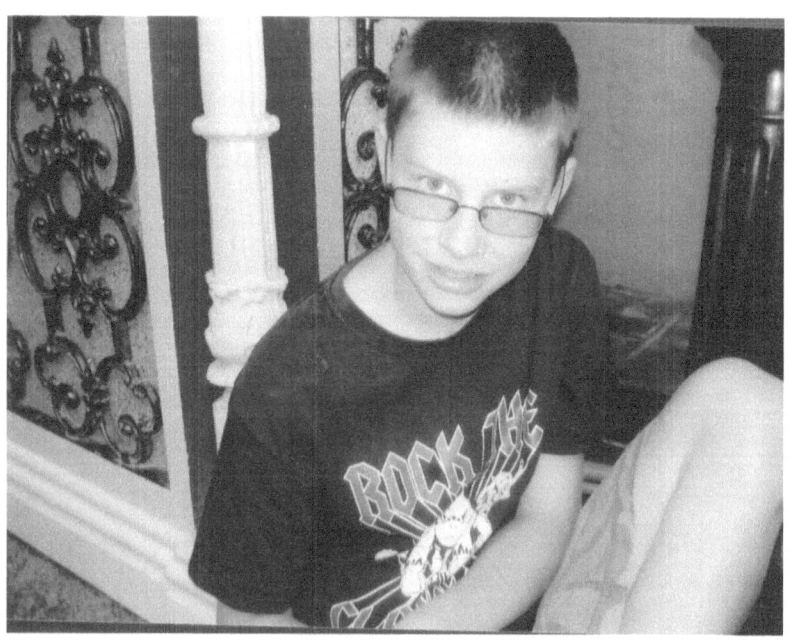

Justin always finds a quiet little corner
Disneyland 2008

Justin Thomas Anderson 2008

Aaron Pollock Anderson 2010

Justin plays bartender 2010

Just me and my favorite gentlemen

Chapter Nine

An Unlikely Superhero

The Champions among us

I learned quite by accident the necessity and the value of being an advocate for my son. I think we all know we will stick up for our kids, but this isn't quite the same as taking their side in an argument. Being a strong advocate doesn't mean I fight his battles. It means I equip him with the tools and skills to fight his own battles. I'm helping to pave the way that is already clear for his peers. Although I might be the reason that he has so much to do in a given day, I'm also why he has great people to help him learn and develop what he needs to grow. Although I might be the invisible source of his frustration, I'm also the one who will make the most difference by the actions I do and don't take.

IEP meetings have gotten considerably easier over the years, but I still play a pivotal role in the ebb and flow of his individual education plan. Recently I went to Justin's fifth grade IEP, which ran smoothly. It has been a long time since I have had to raise much question as to the propositions set forth by the school district. It's still hard to go and listen to how wonderful Justin is but that he just doesn't measure up. That isn't quite how they say it, but it means he can't, won't, should but he doesn't, and shouldn't. It's a continual dialogue, but I am well versed now and at least surrounded by people who truly love my son. That can make all the difference.

Justin may struggle quite a bit, but he does it with a phenomenally positive attitude and great sense of humor. He is very endearing—maybe not to his peers, but the adults in his life love him immensely.

Even his principal, Jane Seelak, has fallen for him and will never quite recover. Jane has become one of Justin's biggest fans at Orange

Avenue Elementary. She has loved getting to know him and has a soft spot for him even though at first she struggled with how to better reach him and really appreciate who he was. Justin, who really loves her, always greets her and introduces her, "Mrs. JaneSeelak," as if her name was all one word.

One day in October, Jane greeted Justin cordially. She had been instructed by the special education director, as had all his teachers, to not encourage Justin to hug them or hold hands. He had developed a habit of doing that, and we were trying to curb it. It might sound benign, but things like that can become a hard pattern to break. At the very least it made him different from his peers because most fifth grade boys didn't hold hands with their teachers. We were trying to help him fit in as best he could. But on that day Justin had heard it was Jane's birthday and greeted her, "Happy Birthday, Mrs. JaneSeelak!" and threw his arms around her in a great bear hug. She couldn't make herself refuse, and so she hugged him right back and enjoyed every second. It became one of her favorite stories to tell.

Justin hasn't always been the only one who needed me to advocate for him. Aaron has run into a snag a time or two as well—albeit he was a lot more straightforward to iron out. For example, in second grade Aaron had an excellent teacher, Mrs. Holly. She was a young, exceedingly pleasant woman with handfuls of curly red hair. She had been a teacher just long enough to recognize Aaron's charm, and we loved her. Unfortunately, for the third year in a row, his teacher got pregnant during the school year. I think they began to believe he was a fertility charm. Once again, Aaron was to be cheated out of a complete year of uninterrupted teaching. But to make matters worse Mrs. Holly was replaced after her husband took an out–of–state job, and she was forced to relocate. The rest of the year was conducted by an ill-equipped long-term substitute who had minimal teaching experience and none with a class of eight-year-olds.

You would think Aaron would catch a break. His kindergarten teacher had disappeared over spring break to have a baby. His first grade teacher was a doll, but she called him Justin by mistake throughout the whole year. (I am pretty sure that kind of spoiled an otherwise memorable year for him. I think it must be tough being Justin's brother sometimes. He is a hard act to follow.) And now Aaron had this long term sub.

For our first parent–teacher conference with the new teacher, Mrs. Groves, I remember balancing in a tiny blue plastic chair as Aaron nervously bopped around the room despite repeated attempts on my part to get him to return to his chair. The new teacher went over what Aaron needed to improve on, starting out by indicating that he was *only* reading one hundred words a minute. I searched my mind for a moment as I had no strong comparison at hand, and Justin, who had huge strengths but definite weaknesses, was not one to whom a comparison would be fair. I cautiously asked what the benchmark should be for reading in second grade. She informed me that he should be reading 120 words per minute by June. Okay, but this was October! For the next twenty minutes she picked apart where he fell short, and as she did, his behavior at the meeting continued to disintegrate. Small wonder.

She finally finished her rendition by asking if I had any questions. Against my better judgment, I heard myself respond, "Yes. What does he do *well?*" She looked completely taken aback and returned to her papers in what seemed a desperate attempt to find something. She did finally say she really liked his attitude toward his friends and classmates. I also asked her what system she had in place to reward positive behavior, so that the kids know when they are doing well. I pointed out to her how much Aaron had heard today about his shortcomings and wondered out loud if any effort to redeem himself would be heralded?

I have no problem hearing where my kids need to see improvements made and being the head of the committee to help them achieve their goals. What I can't abide is pointless banter put together only for the purpose of a meeting. If he needs to make corrections, let's make them, but don't tell me he is lacking a skill that he isn't even expected to know yet. He can't pass a trig test yet either.

Apparently I wasn't the only mother who came away feeling slightly violated. I might not have even been the most outspoken.

Whether it was just the normal course of the year, her peer's help, or maybe even taking some of what we told her to heart, Mrs. Groves made remarkable changes by the time spring conferences rolled around. Her demeanor had changed. She seemed to see things differently and was seeing more from her students than I believe she would have seen otherwise. They seemed to work harder, enjoy learning, and respect her more. I can say that of the teachers I have known, she was the most willing to learn and apply it to her classroom, which was refreshing. Mrs. Groves became Aaron's favorite teacher of all time by the end of the year. What a turnaround that was.

Aaron started third grade in corridors where Justin had never roamed because we moved out of state when Brett was downsized from his job after ten years at the movie studio. We took it as an opportunity to own and operate our own business and relocated up and over the Rockies and into the Centennial State of Colorado.

Aaron made friends quickly, and I don't think I could have gotten him to go to school at all if he didn't have good friends there. Aaron found he still was required to work and remembered that he didn't really enjoy school. Add to that the fact that he hadn't wanted to move in the first place, missed his friends back in California, and was having trouble with the new expectations, rules, and learning systems at his new school, and he was completely overwhelmed. His teacher, Mrs. Baldwin, felt she had Aaron's number and was just going to have to show him who was boss to get his attention. Of course, as seems to usually be the case, she just underlined his resentment.

One evening a little while later, Aaron and I sat on his bed and talked about a particularly rough day. He confided in me through heavy tears that his teacher had pushed the back of his head in an attempt to move him more quickly toward the door. As he told it, he had gone out for recess with all the other kids when a little boy came to get him. The boy told him Mrs. Baldwin needed to see him. He went to the room, and she told him his class work wasn't sufficiently completed and sent him back to his desk with a bit of a shove to the back of his head. From the way he cried, I could tell he felt debased and betrayed because teachers weren't supposed to be cruel. He did as he was told but never got over that injustice and never forgave her for her misstep.

I showed up to school the next day and spoke with the principal and school psychologist. I explained the difficulties that the teacher had described. I told them about how he wasn't getting his work done. How he was not focusing well in her class and how he was falling further behind all the time. I suggested that we consider modifications if necessary and I requested assessments be done and signed a release for Aaron's previous IEP to be sent, but nothing ever came of those requests. I sat in on the class to help out and made my presence known, but I never heard another bad thing. From then on, Mrs. Baldwin was very quick to tell me how well Aaron was doing and how much his behavior had improved. I have my doubts about that though because Aaron is true to his soul and hasn't changed. I suspect she probably just realized he wasn't as easy to pick on as she thought he might be. Or perhaps she just doesn't understand who he is. What a shame because she missed out on so much.

Part of being an advocate is knowing who your child is and celebrating that knowledge by sharing it with others. I have tried to show my boys, as well as my husband, how special each of them is. I try to help Brett understand the boys better when they seem inexplicably difficult and that who they are isn't an accident. The boys are just who they are meant to be.

I have learned from my children that there is no greater joy than championing someone who hasn't really found his own voice yet. Being supportive at home is one thing, but showing that special person, and those who know him, just what he means to me is a whole other ballgame. That has meant many conversations, many interrupted days, and many desperate prayers. I have tried to show my family that I hold them dearer than anything else and that my heart is filled with everything they are and all they want to become. So when Justin says, "Hey, can I tell you something?" you can bet there isn't anything more important than listening to what he wants to share. We all need someone to believe in as a reason to keep up the good fight. I am proud to be among those who are champions for my sons.

I find that these heroes are found in the most unlikely places—the principal who knows that some days when Justin is sent to talk to her, the best solution is to just share lunch together; the aide who knows him so well that she understands emotions that don't seem to make sense to anyone else, like that he is angry because of a grudge he carries from possibly quite a while ago; the teacher who offers to ride the bus home with him so he won't get off at the wrong stop on his first day; the best friends who invent ongoing Star Wars sagas in the play yard at school and make school bearable; the brother who watches out for you even though they are years younger than you, helps rebuild broken Legos, and pats your head in church because it is in their lap even though it doesn't belong there. For me, they are the little boys who show you how a different world works, one you otherwise couldn't have found. These heroes make such a difference.

There is a picture that sits atop Justin's dresser of another unlikely superhero:

Super Wombat! He watches down over us in his blue tights and flailing red cape.

He reminds us that heroes don't always look like you might expect, and sometimes they come in clever disguise. Super Wombat rose out of the mind's eye of a child who, not so long ago couldn't access his imagination. He was born by the hands of a child who hates to write or draw because of the complexity of the movements that leave him disappointed. He has undoubtedly been through numerous triumphs and tribulations, but I fear he has all but retired now. Still, he watches over us and reminds me that there is so much I still have to learn about what these little boys of mine have to offer. *What greatness is still locked up and waiting to be born?* I wonder.

Super Wombat, from on high, reminds me to watch out for unlikely heroes, and he reminds me I live among them.

Chapter Ten

Bittersweet

The Delicious Agony of Progress

It's the evening of Justin's final Cub Scout graduation. He is ten years old and aloft with pride. I'm standing here alone even though friends and family surround me. Like so often, I feel that even though there's an undeniable buzz around me and I'm bombarded with well wishes and excitement, I'm nonetheless alone in the understanding of just what it took to get here tonight. But I'm blessed to know something like this so intimately.

Justin has been involved in Cub Scouts almost four years, and it has been a great trip. He has made friends here and he has learned a lot of great things. Tonight is the Arrow of Light Ceremony, where these scouts will be awarded the Arrow of Light, a symbol that consists of an arrow pointing the way to a good life and a rising sun, which represents the constant new challenges provided by life This honor is much more difficult to obtain than any belt loop, activity badge, or rank patches. To obtain this award, scouts meet many requirements, including the completion of eight activity badges over an eighteen-month period; participation in camps, hikes, and activities; and the memorization of the Scout Oath and Scout Law. This is the last and greatest award a Cub Scout can achieve.

For the ceremony Justin is adorned in all his den and pack activity badges. Pins and colors hang proudly from his uniform. The fleur-de-lis on its tartan backdrop encircles his collar, and his belt boasts symbols of nearly four years of completed tasks. Tonight, he and his fellow Webelos will watch while the archer draws back the arrows, each hand-painted to represent their individual accomplishments. They will grin as they watch their arrows soar, one by one, and hit their mark in the target. The boys will take one final stroll across the bridge that they have crossed every year during their promotion of rank. It is bittersweet.

Aaron is here tonight as well with his Wolf den. He proudly wears his uniform, which will shortly bear a wolf emblem. He has worked hard this year to achieve his rank and understands how much is required of a scout to achieve an "Arrow of Light" like his brother will do tonight.

It is a beautifully crisp California, February evening. The sun is setting, and the families begin to file into the cafeteria of our elementary school. Our den has been setting up for this evening's event all afternoon. The tables are draped in the Scout colors of blue and gold. Pine boughs run along the center of the table, and pinecones, generously provided by the big trees outside, are scattered among the branches. In the center of each table is a picture of one of the Scouts who will graduate tonight. The rough wooden frames encase the images of these boys who look so grown to us now—and yet they are not.

Dinner is the usual catered affair, and for the third year in a row, I stand in line with my plastic plate and wait to have it filled with marginal food for my birthday dinner. Somehow the end of February always hosts this age-old event, and somehow it always falls on my birthday. At least the company is warm and energy is wonderful. Yellow and blue balloons bob around the corners of the room and memory books for each of the graduates are laid out for us to scribble remembrances for them. A target awaits its duty up on the stage and the designated "Indian" archers traipse in.

Brett took the evening off to be with us here tonight. He proudly watches our son and we share a mutual anxiety and energy. We are unsure how Justin will handle all this excitement. Brett is trying to accept Justin for his endearing and quirky manner. He recognizes his shortcomings and sees them as characteristics, not faults. He is beginning to see just how much fortitude and inner power it takes to be Justin. Brett is learning to find strength and confidence in himself that allows for the luxury of such personal growth.

Brett and I try to politely fold ourselves into these impossibly small tables and benches meant for the elementary school children. We become intimately acquainted with those we thought we had known well enough before and boldly introduce ourselves to those with whom we had not previously shared this privilege. With our elbows pinned to our sides, we attempt to remove roasted chicken from its frame with a flimsy plastic fork and knife, escort a slippery bite of salad to our hopeful palate, and try to absorb the overdiluted mashed potatoes with the cold wheat roll while the slideshow begins above the stage.

Well-scripted music accompanies the images of our children through these last few years. Less than a dozen kids will be recognized tonight, but everyone shares in the glory because they realize their moment is coming as well. We watch the still pictures of beaming faces, muddy hikes, chilly campouts, and gritty pinewood derby races. We see things we had forgotten and things we wish we could. We see the boys in old uniforms that they have long since outgrown both physically and emotionally. We see them cheering each other on and helping each other grow. We see the progress and the spirit that each of them embodies. I realize that this moment is so long awaited yet so fleeting.

The boys from the Cobra Den march up on the stage, and the ceremony progresses until each of them has been recognized sufficiently and each of them has added their own personality to the evening. They are each asked to read a short passage before they cross over the bridge one last time. I pray that Justin only reads from the card and doesn't choose now to take advantage of his captive audience and the fact that Mom and Dad are wedged into their seats. He raises his hand, and I cringe because I'm completely aware that I'm much too far away to field a question from him and he's determined to interject. *Lord, what is he going to say out loud before I can stop him?*

A moment later, I am relieved when I realize he is on script tonight. My heart settles back into rhythm. He has been known to veer dramatically off course from time to time, and I know this looks like a grand opportunity to host a round of Jeopardy. I'm sure I can see that thought flicker through his mind, but he regains his focus and plays his role just a bit more exuberantly than the rest.

There are thirty-six-inch wooden arrows, each marked specifically for one of the boys. Each arrow bears the colored bands that correlate with things the boys have achieved throughout their careers as scouts. The archer, in full headdress, takes the stage and one by one the arrows slice through the air and hit their target squarely. The audience sounds its approval, and the boys remove their arrows and are recognized one last time as Cub Scouts.

The boys follow the close of this ceremony with the anticipation of another. They will all be promoted from elementary school and forever leave behind this magical age of innocence. They will embark too soon into the channels of middle school and trade in the tooth fairy for MTV. They will stop listening for reindeer hooves and start listening to their ever-changing hormones. How desperately I want them to hold on to their naivety for a little while longer because there are simply some things that can never be replaced or regained once they are gone.

I have dreaded this moment for many years. From the minute Justin began kindergarten at Orange Avenue Elementary surrounded by this excellent team of professionals, I have worried about the day he would leave. He has made so much progress here. It's bittersweet to see Justin here today, but his accomplishments and his tireless efforts have afforded it to him. There are so many paradoxical feelings wrapped up in this ceremony. I feel so elated and so tearful. I'm thrilled beyond words at how far he has come, I'm sorry to be leaving such a welcome place, and I'm apprehensive about what lies ahead.

Together Brett and I look on with pride as Justin prepares to walk across the outdoor stage. These are monumental times. We remember the work it has taken us all to get to this point as a family. This is the end of Justin's term in elementary school and the end of our lives on California's coast.

A few months later in late June, Justin stands in the blazing morning sun this day with all of his peers. Justin was sick with the flu the previous night and is pale and exhausted, but he wouldn't have missed this for the world. It has taken six years, four different aides, three principals, dozens of therapists and paraprofessionals, and one very determined and tireless family to get to this moment.

I watch Justin, and after a very long night he is listless, but he is dapper. He is quiet, but he shines. He is adorned in his new black slacks, black patent leather loafers, a long-sleeved blue tailored shirt, and a black belt, all set off by a deep blue and soft yellow necktie. As his name is called, he crosses the outside stage and shakes hands with Mr. Noble, the principal. Justin smiles but looks at the ground. He is very happy and very proud, but the overwhelming heat, crackling speakers, and emotions make it impossible for him to look at his congratulator. He is trying to close out some of the sensations, and visual images are the easiest to stop.

For once I'm not alone. Brett and I are standing with Ms. Kathy, Justin's steadfast, unyielding, and enamored aide for the last three years and my friend; his resource teacher, Mrs. Ali, who has helped us for all six years; and "Mrs. JaneSeelak," who has thankfully crashed the festivities to offer her congratulations to the fifth graders she had come to know so well in the four years they were all together. These women alone perhaps understand just what it took to get to this point. They were there every minute—when things went wrong as well as when they went right. They helped Justin back over the fence when he wanted to run away. They helped him find friends and participate in games. They helped him make his work legible. They helped him survive the perils of the playground and the labyrinth of school's expectations. These women, Justin's teachers and my friends, share what this means with us, and they're just as elated and simultaneously heartbroken to watch him cross the stage.

As I watch Justin, I know that he isn't the only one who has come through obstacles but in my opinion nobody has started with so little and gained so much. Nobody has put more into his own growth. Nobody has worked harder for as long as he has. Nobody has experienced so much personal pain of self-recognition. There are many who have made more friends, have had better grades, have better penmanship, and are more articulate or athletic. There are even a few who have all of those qualities, but not one of them has had to work as hard as Justin has.

His victory is his own, but I will relish in it just a bit myself—and I'm in good company in this remarkable occasion.

Chapter Eleven

Accidentally Beautiful

Finding Beauty in Unexpected Places

Following our move, sixth grade has been quite a challenge for Justin, but he generally still enjoys school even though it is hard for him to make friends and there are many new things he has to learn. Middle school brings all kinds of firsts. You have to get used to lockers with complicated locks, many different classes, changing for P.E. in front of everyone, and a whole new set of expectations.

There are certain things that make Justin noticeably different from the other kids. Justin still has an aide to help when he needs it, but the aide follows a small group of kids to their classes to assist the teacher when necessary instead of working with Justin one on one. He has a different lock on his locker, but all in all, he fits in very well.

At eleven and a half years old, Justin has started approaching puberty well before I expected it, and the "bikini girl" talk is a daily topic these days. He is interested in things that are way out of my and his father's comfort zone strangely enough. I don't want him to feel like what he's thinking about is bad or wrong, but I just want him not to think about it at all yet! That isn't too much to ask, is it? His aide at school has fast become my rock and sounding board, so when underwire became the topic of our dinner conversation, it prompted this e-mail to her:

I am *not* going to survive puberty! And he's only eleven. I had to put parental controls on the computer last night. He's looking up "bikini girls." Have you seen some of the bikinis out there? My Victoria's Secret catalogue never even made it in the house yesterday. It went right into the recycle bin.

He decided underwire was the topic of last night's dinner table discussion. Explain that one without losing it. I really didn't want to talk about bras and why some need more support than others! I asked him if he had any questions, and he just had comments. He said he likes "the waist, the hair, the breasts (guess we knew that!), the eyes, and the belly button." He asked if belly buttons were "required." I think he meant to ask if everyone has one. I told him what it was.

You will remember our talking about encouraging reading books that have more value than Calvin and Hobbes when we spoke about it at the IEP last week? Well, I felt triumphant because I got him to pick up a book with some value. He grabbed his *Human Body Book*, the one that came with a plastic human body model that you put all the pieces in. I let him read for half an hour or so and then went in to tell him good night, and he pipes up, "I didn't know my private parts made babies!"

Damn it! Where did I put that Pokemon book?!

HELP!

There is never a dull moment around here. Now, I wonder how I am going to keep Justin from discussing his newfound interest with Aaron. Ever tried spitting into the wind? Success seems about as likely as that. Let's mix intellect, hormones, and social misinterpretation together and see what shakes out! Eight years ago the behaviorist was right when she said Justin was going to be a "fun teenager." I've still not forgiven her for that little premonition.

The boys are grinding through the difficulties of leaving behind every friend and loved one. This is by far the biggest challenge we have faced as a family. We are once again growing. We feel a bit alone here some days, but we have met some nice people and commiserate with them over the tribulations of being a California transplant in a state that actually has *weather*. We are fully aware of why we changed the tires on the car back in October. We understand why we go and shovel snow even though it is still falling. We know what it feels like when the car slips on the ice; the ratcheting of the anti-lock braking system is as common a sound now as the chatter in the backseat. (Funny, it isn't all that different from many other slippery situations in which I have found myself.) And we know what it feels like to be waiting for spring to settle warmly over the earth.

As Aaron settles into third grade, he's one of the youngest in his class, and he amazes me. He has such a way with friends, and I am captivated at how easy he makes it look. I'm not even sure what quality it is that comes so naturally to him. He is kind and inviting with the kids, but it's more than that. There is just a pleasant and open invitation that he exudes. Part of me really wants to say, "It's the age. If you like Star Wars and so does the next guy, then boom, you're friends!" But that's not so. I know it's far more complicated than that.

Aaron has some wonderful friends with whom he engages mostly, he has friends he invites over and whose homes he visits, but he also reaches out to those kids who are more difficult to befriend—to the kids who need it most. At times, this has even alienated him from other friends, but he perseveres. He has a heart of gold and will of steel. He knows how hard it can be for some kids to make friends, and he enjoys being there for them.

So much has happened this year. I'm sure that those little acorns that I found in Aaron's pockets not so many months ago have sprouted and are well on their way to becoming great strong creations that will weather life's storms and give support to the delicate world around them. It's a reflection, I hope, of all the seeds I have tried to plant in my family. We have crossed the Continental Divide, and we have begun to put roots down here on the east side of the beautiful snow-capped Rockies. The windows of our home no longer frame a garden of perpetual roses but instead watch the aspens turn to amber and then give way to swirling snowflakes as the mercury shimmers somewhere south of the midline.

I found our box of what Southern Californians call "going to the snow" clothes, which are now just clothes to be worn this time of year. I have found that one pair of gloves and one jacket aren't enough, and you can't really go without if you misplace one. I know what minus-six Fahrenheit feels like, and I know what the gale-force, icy wind feels like when it sneaks through every crevice around the windows. We have watched spectacular lightning flash across the reservoir and the street and cowered when the thunder gets so close it feels like the house might split in two. We know what it means to be snowed in. We have witnessed when three feet of snow is built up against every door, and we know what it's like to realize that for weeks at a time, it would be easier to ski down your street than to attempt to get the car over all the ice.

Our new business is just getting its wings. Brett is flourishing in this enormous undertaking, and I'm trying not to drown. Brett found a business opportunity in Houston, Texas, a specialty store that sells NASA souvenirs and memorabilia—TheSpaceStore.com—and relocated it to our neck of the woods. The store has products ranging from clothing, posters, books, solar system images, and games to costumes, dehydrated food, meteorites, shuttle tiles, and autographed paraphernalia. We are even lucky enough to have some items that have been flown in space. Neither Brett, nor I have ever owned a business even though both of us have some experience working in the trenches of businesses that we felt were like they were partly ours. We are still treading lightly over unfamiliar ground but every day we find we are a little surer of ourselves.

The business continues to flourish hopefully because of us but probably sometimes in spite of us. Brett is enjoying the amount of thought, care, and attention that has to go into the business. He lights up when he sees the difference he has been able to make. The brilliant growth he has been able to forge in the Space Store still pales in comparison to the growth that he has realized for himself, but the Space Store is just what he needed. It's computer and Internet based, fun, complicated, and educational.

It's amazing to look back just three years ago and ponder how far we have all come individually and as a family. It seems almost unheard of to survive such trials in today's world, but it is well worth the fight.

Brett has grown into the man I think he always wanted and needed to be. We spend a lot more time together. He no longer works the night shift unless he wants to. He can attend all those things he used to miss out on with the boys and me. Brett and I spend four or five hours a day working with each other, and then I leave to pick up the boys and carry on with the day, the house, the yard, and the extracurricular. Brett makes time to take Aaron to scouts and Justin on overnighter field trips. He makes plans to take me out for my birthday in addition to the Cub Scout Gala. He makes plans to take Aaron, who dumped the Kings for the Avalanche, to an Avs game and Justin to a Rockies game when the Los Angeles Dodgers are in town. Justin is a California kid at heart!

At one time Brett's absence was so complete that I don't think the boys had any idea what their dad was really like, but now they know him as well as they know themselves. Brett is a constant connected force in the boys' lives. He's home for dinner and bedtime, he's able to see soccer games, he watches Justin's Taekwondo belt tests, and he goes to bed with me every night. He is a parent, a confidant, and an ally in the trials and tribulations of growing up.

Aaron, at nine, lives to play imaginary games with his friends. He loves to lie in bed at night with me and listen to me read him fantastic stories of grand adventure and magic. He still bounces off the walls at times, but he is getting better at landing on solid ground. Although he made it mandatory that I locate the Urgent Care quickly as blood poured from his split chin following a game of tag at Cub Scouts, eight stitches later he had yet another scar to share with his friends.

He's the little brother around here, but his role seems more divided. He has taken on the task of his brother's keeper. I try to let him know that even though I appreciate his fortitude in the matter, it really isn't his job to make sure nothing goes wrong because there is a fine line between looking out for each other and becoming the warden. I have come to realize that being the big brother has little to do with chronological age. I try to remind Aaron that he is Justin's brother, not his parent. Justin already has enough of those around.

Justin has always been a very good patient. Though he is often long winded in his very complete answers he tries to give the doctors. We recently had an appointment at the pediatrician's office and Justin and I were discussing the efficacy of his medications with the good doctor. After making a few minor alterations in the dosing, the doctor suggested that I consider updating Justin's vaccinations. He indicated that he should have a vaccine to protect him from meningitis as well as the adult form of whooping cough.

I explained to Justin what the shots were for. I told him clearly that there were a couple of diseases that were very dangerous and even deadly. I told him that if he took the shots, he would have immunity and be safe. He likes the word *immunity*.

He thrust out his arm and boldly stated, "I am ready to face death!"

He meant he was willing to submit to the shots, so he could safely face the diseases that he might encounter. It was a bit dramatic, but at least he was willing.

He sat quietly for a few minutes and then very matter-of-factly asked, "Will it make me normal?"

The question just hung heavily in the room for a minute. I swallowed hard, fighting back the tears that threatened to spill down my cheeks at any moment, and tried to refill the air in my lungs that had just rushed out. Little blacks spots danced in my eyes for a second while I weighed my answer.

"What do you mean?"

Justin replied, "I'm different. Will the shots make me like everyone else?"

To clarify, I asked, "Do you mean will they make you *not autistic*?"

He answered, "Yes."

I drew a shaky breath that I hoped was silent. I closed my eyes, praying for words to come, and replied honestly, "No, Justin. Nothing can do that." I paused and added, "Tell me something though if there *was* such a shot, if something *could* do that, would you *want* to be just like everyone else (I tried to make my tone of voice flat and dull), *or* do you like… who… you… are?"

I held my breath awaiting his reply. It came swiftly and confidently.

"I *like* who I am!"

He seemed almost relieved. I know I was.

That boy can still yank the proverbial rug right out from under me. When I least expect it, he's sad because our new kitten will only get to see him for six years because when he's eighteen he has to leave. The notion seems firmly planted in his mind and is disturbing for him. I promise no one ever told him that at our house, and it is something I am trying to undermine. I remind him his uncle is thirty-six years old and still has yet to move out of his mother's house. But somehow logic strikes me: He's right because he's three fourths of the way to being an adult in the legal sense and six years seems so brief.

One of the classes Justin took as an elective this year couldn't have been more telling. His teacher chose three-dimensional art as an elective for him. The class has involved him in creating structures out of clay. His first project was to work the clay into a cup and prepare it for the kiln. For many days he worked on the project. And for many days he drove his teachers mad because he used too much clay and didn't work it down thin enough. He had a plan from which he couldn't be diverted.

When the project neared completion, he told me that his cup was more of a bowl and that he had added more to it than he was supposed to. His teacher confided in me that the class had been a huge challenge for both of them because Justin had been fairly obstinate throughout the process. I let her know how big a deal it was that he had been able to do it at all, how he had been completely unable to tolerate media such as this for most of his life, and how poor his fine motor skills are at precision. I then described past scenarios of any project involving liquid glue or finger paint that had ended in disasters and many trips to the sink to wash and rewash his hands. He simply couldn't stand the sensation on his hands, but I let her know, too, that I would remind him that he needed to be respectful even if he didn't like it.

The bowl project seemed to go on for quite a while. He worked at this task for weeks, forming and reforming. Once the bowl had taken on the shape that he had decided it should be, he then was able to add the color. I'm not sure if he didn't like how the colors looked as he applied them or if he was experimenting with them all, but many applications of glaze flowed over the surfaces of this chalice before he was finished. Finally, it was placed in the kiln and fired although he was warned that it might explode due to the nature of its thickened structure. I think the teacher considered it a minor miracle that it hadn't shattered in the kiln's heat because it probably shouldn't have survived the process, but it did.

I think even Justin might have been surprised to see it in one piece. He described to me how he made it, then how he added all the colors, and that the final result he said was "a color I can only describe as sea blue." As he held it aloft on the palm of his hand to present it to me, he softly affirmed that it was "accidentally beautiful."

How ironic, how completely accurate, and how profoundly simple that Justin himself summed up in two words what might take an exhaustive breath to describe. Everything Justin achieves and what we have become as a family is indeed accidentally beautiful. As a family we learned how to cope with fathoms of autism and enjoy its unexpected charm. We've learned how to navigate through the intermingling and varying degrees of sensitivities and attention deficits that affect both boys and sometimes Brett and me as well. We've been artful and cunning, we've been creative and flexible, we've been forgiving and accepting, and we've learned life lessons from these young masters of the program. As a family we have survived depression, illness, loss, unemployment, and separation. We survived a demoralizing layoff and a long-distance move away from everything that we had ever known and come to love so dearly. We have grown through every experience that we thought might have torn us apart.

I'm sure that the things we face in our lives are by no means an accident. The way we choose to respond to obstacles, disillusionment, and pain will become the footing by which we will progress into the next opportunity. I'm not pretending that every path we have chosen was the right one. I don't know if every session of every therapy had merit. And I'm sure that for every great move I have made as a wife and mother, there have been countless flubs and missteps. And yet, the striking resilience and undaunted fortitude with which this family keeps stepping forward is inspiring. It's my conclusion that as is so often the case, Justin is once again correct. What sits before us now could only accurately be described as "accidentally beautiful."

Afterword

I am not a particularly bold person. I tend to avoid inflaming situations or rocking the boat. I am generally pretty easy-going, especially when it comes to matters concerning myself. I'm strong but also fairly inconspicuous. It wasn't until I felt my child was in danger that I felt something stir in my soul. Justin was in danger of becoming isolated and failing to make strides in development and emotional connection. At times I felt like no one knew what to do, not even the professionals whom we all come to trust. It became my focus and my goal to provide Justin and later Aaron with the foundation they required. My children have given me cause to find my voice. It is through them that I have found my footing in this world. They have helped me to find the God-given strength that I didn't know I had. They have required me to be a better person than I would have been on my own.

Each time I thought that my world had shattered, I discovered it hadn't. I discovered I had the fortitude, will, courage, and strength to meet each new battle, and each new battle seemed to prime me all the more for the next. Every time I needed them, I found I had been equipped with the tools and the energy that I needed to persevere and triumph over whatever lay before me. My children have required me to be more diverse and more confident than I knew how to be when we started down this path. I owe them a great debt for that.

Battles will continue to rage. From time to time, I will get that phone call confirming that Justin mooned the class or that he removed himself from a noisy environment and hid in the bathroom for twenty minutes until he completed his work in a quieter place while the teachers turned the school upside-down looking for him. Occasionally, Aaron will still lash out in anger and aggression because his video game didn't go the way he wanted it to, and he will continue to milk every last second out of every day in an attempt to thwart bedtime for just a while longer. However, I remain in awe of just who my children are becoming. Life is an expedition, a journey of discovery and growth. When Justin leaves the noisy classroom, it isn't so much that he left as it is that he recognized his own fading tolerance limit. He opted to remove himself from an intolerable situation before he lost control of his temper. When Aaron has trouble going to sleep at night, it is because there is so much going on his mind, not because he intends to misbehave.

I remind myself as often as I can to consider who my children are and the strides they have already made. I remind myself that there is a reason behind every altercation that I need to figure out if I want to turn the tide and solve the problem. It is an ongoing challenge, but one I welcome and even relish. I find great satisfaction in knowing that my husband and I are responsible in shaping these young lives and in honing their many skills and strengths while minimizing the things that challenge them most.

I look forward to tomorrow. There is always an unexpected flash of brilliance—a moment that transcends all else. That moment is something that holds the world still for me briefly. Sometimes I have to look harder than others. Sometimes the reward is very small, but it is always there. I choose to hold on to those, write them down, and build my days around them. Then these moments will be the strength that I will draw from when skies turn black and the brilliance seems a distant memory. They will remind me why this life we know so well and have come to love so dearly is truly accidentally beautiful!

References

(1) Autism and Developmental Disabilities Monitoring Network –publication of the Center for Disease Control. Community Report 2009.

(2) http://www.cdc.gov/ncbddd/autism/documents/ AutismCommunityReport.pdf

(3) Center for Disease Control; Morbidity and Mortality Weekly Report; December 18, 2009/volume 58/ No. SS-10

(4) Center for Disease Control –Cerebral Palsy

(5) National Institute of Health. Eunice Kennedy Shriver National Institute of Child Health and Human Development

(6) Tony Attwood-Published Papers- The Pattern of Abilities and Development of Girls with Asperger's Syndrome

www.ingramcontent.com/pod-product-compliance
Lightning Source LLC
Chambersburg PA
CBHW020247290526
45784CB00003B/1127

* 9 7 8 0 5 5 7 7 6 4 3 1 0 *